COMPREHENSIVE RESEARCH
AND STUDY GUIDE

BLOOM'S
MAJOR
SHORT STORY
WRITERS

Rudyard

Kipling

EDITED AND WITH AN
INTRODUCTION BY HAROLD BLOOM

CURRENTLY AVAILABLE

BLOOM'S MAJOR
SHORT STORY WRITERS

Sherwood Anderson
Isaac Babel
Jorge Luis Borges
Italo Calvino
Raymond Carver
John Cheever
Anton Chekhov
Joseph Conrad
Julio Cortázar
Stephen Crane
William Faulkner
F. Scott Fitzgerald
Nikolai Gogol
Nathaniel Hawthorne
Ernest Hemingway
O. Henry
Shirley Jackson
Henry James
James Joyce
Franz Kafka
Rudyard Kipling
D.H. Lawrence
Jack London
Thomas Mann
Guy de Maupassant
Herman Melville
Flannery O'Connor
Edgar Allan Poe
Katherine Anne Porter
J.D. Salinger
John Steinbeck
Mark Twain
John Updike
Eudora Welty

COMPREHENSIVE RESEARCH
AND STUDY GUIDE

BLOOM'S
MAJOR
SHORT
STORY
WRITERS

Rudyard Kipling

CHELSEA HOUSE
PUBLISHERS
A Haights Cross Communications Company

Philadelphia

EDITED AND WITH AN INTRODUCTION BY HAROLD BLOOM

First Printing
1 3 5 7 9 8 6 4 2

Library of Congress Cataloging-in-Publication Data

Rudyard Kipling / edited with an introduction by Harold Bloom.
     p. cm. — (Bloom's major short story writers)
Includes bibliographical references (p.   ) and index.
  ISBN 0-7910-7591-5
1. Kipling, Rudyard, 1865–1936—Criticism and interpretation. I.
Bloom, Harold. II. Title. III. Series.
  PR4857.R77 2003
  828'.809—dc21
                                                            2003011588

Chelsea House Publishers
1974 Sproul Road, Suite 400
Broomall, PA 19008-0914

www.chelseahouse.com

Contributing Editor: Michael Baughan

Cover design by Keith Trego

Layout by EJB Publishing Services

CONTENTS

USER'S GUIDE

This volume is designed to present biographical, critical, and bibliographical information on the author and the author's best-known or most important short stories. Following Harold Bloom's editor's note and introduction is a concise biography of the author that discusses major life events and important literary accomplishments. A critical analysis of each story follows, tracing significant themes, patterns, and motifs in the work. An annotated list of characters supplies brief information on the main characters in each story.

A selection of critical extracts, derived from previously published material, follows each thematic analysis. In most cases, these extracts represent the best analysis available from a number of leading critics. Because these extracts are derived from previously published material, they will include the original notations and references when available. Each extract is cited, and readers are encouraged to use the original publications as they continue their research. A bibliography of the author's writings, a list of additional books and articles on the author and their work, and an index of themes and ideas conclude the volume.

As with any study guide, this volume is designed as a supplement to the works being discussed, and is in no way intended as a replacement for those works. The reader is advised to read the text prior to using this study guide, and to keep it accessible for quick reference.

ABOUT THE EDITOR

Harold Bloom is Sterling Professor of the Humanities at Yale University and Henry W. and Albert A. Berg Professor of English at the New York University Graduate School. He is the author of over 20 books, and the editor of more than 30 anthologies of literary criticism.

Professor Bloom's works include *Shelley's Mythmaking* (1959), *The Visionary Company* (1961), *Blake's Apocalypse* (1963), *Yeats* (1970), *A Map of Misreading* (1975), *Kabbalah and Criticism* (1975), *Agon: Toward a Theory of Revisionism* (1982), *The American Religion* (1992), *The Western Canon* (1994), and *Omens of Millennium: The Gnosis of Angels, Dreams, and Resurrection* (1996). *The Anxiety of Influence* (1973) sets forth Professor Bloom's provocative theory of the literary relationships between the great writers and their predecessors. His most recent books include *Shakespeare: The Invention of the Human*, a 1998 National Book Award finalist, *How to Read and Why* (2000), and *Genius: A Mosaic of One Hundred Exemplary Creative Minds* (2002).

Professor Bloom earned his Ph.D. from Yale University in 1955 and has served on the Yale faculty since then. He is a 1985 MacArthur Foundation Award recipient and served as the Charles Eliot Norton Professor of Poetry at Harvard University in 1987–88. In 1999 he was awarded the prestigious American Academy of Arts and Letters Gold Medal for Criticism. Professor Bloom is the editor of several other Chelsea House series in literary criticism, including BLOOM'S MAJOR SHORT STORY WRITERS, BLOOM'S MAJOR NOVELISTS, BLOOM'S MAJOR DRAMATISTS, BLOOM'S MODERN CRITICAL INTERPRETATIONS, BLOOM'S MODERN CRITICAL VIEWS, and BLOOM'S BIOCRITIQUES.

EDITOR'S NOTE

My Introduction comments briefly upon the five stories covered in this volume, and also considers other stories, one from the *Just So* sequence, as well as "Mary Postgate," among the later works.

The rightly renowned "The Man Who Would Be King" is very usefully studied by Paul Fussell in the context of Masonry, and by Thomas A. Shippey and Michael Short in its technical aspects.

"Without Benefit of Clergy" is eloquently interpreted by the late Elliot Gilbert as an elegiac testimonial to the transcendence of love over rituals both social and religious.

In another superb exegesis, John A. McClure juxtaposes Kipling's heroine in "Lispeth" with her reappearance in Kipling's masterpiece, *Kim*.

"The Church That Was at Antioch" is viewed by the novelist Angus Wilson as an exposition of Kipling's personal fusion of humanism and Christianity.

Much the most puzzling of these stories, "Mrs. Bathurst" receives distinguished commentaries from the novelist David Lodge, and the eminent critic, John Bayley.

INTRODUCTION
Harold Bloom

Kipling was a superb short story writer, who developed a defensive array of narrative devices that sometimes enhanced his fundamental vitality as an author, and at other moments perhaps impeded him. His art in later stories is extraordinarily subtle, marking his transition from the novel *Kim*, deeply influenced by Mark Twain, to oblique modes that seem to have been affected by Joseph Conrad and Henry James.

"The Man Who Would Be King" is probably Kipling's most popular story, and the public response is validly based upon the skilled, vivid characterization of the protagonists, Carnehan and Dravot. I myself find it difficult to endorse the general critical judgment that this story is an ambivalent allegory of British colonialism. Though ironical throughout, "The Man Who Would Be King" essentially is a celebration of the flamboyance and audacity of Carnehan and Dravot.

The erotic ironies of "Without Benefit of Clergy" and of "Lispeth" are tempered by what could be termed Kipling's own nostalgia for an erotic idealism that had deserted him. Ameera and Lispeth are antithetical to one another, in a contrast that depends as much upon personality as on their diverse experiences of British love. Kipling is sage enough to show us that Ameera's fulfilled nature nevertheless provokes an early death, whereas Lispeth's survival (into *Kim*) is secured by her bitterness.

Kipling's remarkable originality as storyteller triumphs in "The Church That Was At Antioch," which is composed in a marvelous prose, very much Kipling's invention:

> There filed out from behind the Little Circus four blaring trumpets, a standard, and a dozen Mounted Police. Their wise little grey Arabs sidled, passaged, shouldered, and nosed softly into the mob, as though they wanted petting, while the trumpets deafened the narrow street. An open square, near by, eased the pressure before long. Here the Patrol broke into fours, and gridironed it, saluting the images of the gods at each corner and in the

centre. People stopped, as usual, to watch how cleverly the incense was cast down over the withers into the spouting cressets; children reached up to pat horses which they said they knew; family groups re-found each other in the smoky dusk; hawkers offered cooked suppers; and soon the crowd melted into the main traffic avenues.

That is a very different instrument than the prose of *Huckleberry Finn* or of the earlier Henry James. Kipling writes a middle style that *seems* timeless but of course consciously inaugurates the inception of the Twentieth century. It is an apparently plain prose that intimates a hovering darkness, as here at the close of a true shocker, "Mary Postgate":

> *But* it was a fact. A woman who had missed these things could still be useful—more useful than a man in certain respects. She thumped like a pavoir through the settling ashes at the secret thrill of it. The rain was damping the fire, but she could feel—it was too dark to see—that her work was done. There was a dull red glow at the bottom of the destructor, not enough to char the wooden lid if she slipped it half over against the driving wet. This arranged, she leaned on the poker and waited, while an increasing rapture laid hold on her. She ceased to think. She gave herself up to feel. Her long pleasure was broken by a sound that she had waited for in agony several times in her life. She leaned forward and listened, smiling. There could be no mistake. She closed her eyes and drank it in. Once it ceased abruptly.

> "Go on," she murmured, half aloud. "That isn't the end."

> Then the end came very distinctly in a lull between two rain-gusts. Mary Postgate drew her breath short between her teeth and shivered from head to foot. "*That's* all right," said she contentedly, and went up to the house, where she scandalised the whole routine by taking a luxurious hot bath before tea, and came down

looking, as Miss Fowler said when she saw her lying all relaxed on the other sofa, "quite handsome!"

With refined sadistic sexuality, Mary Postgate thus enjoys the slow death of a downed, badly wounded German aviator, whose agony in the shrubbery revitalizes *her*. Kipling perhaps does too much of the work for the reader, but we shudder anyway at his art. It achieves a more equivocal triumph in "Mrs. Bathurst," where we are bewildered yet suborned by indirect narrations, which come to seem more important than the dark eros that has destroyed the tale's protagonists.

When I was a child, I delighted in the *Just So Stories*, which go on sustaining me in old age. How could one improve the close of "The Cat That Walked By Himself":

> Then the Man threw his two books and his little stone axe (that makes three) at the Cat, and the Cat ran out of the Cave and the Dog chased him up a tree; and from that day to this, Best Beloved, three proper Men out of five will always throw things at a Cat whenever they meet him, and all proper Dogs will chase him up a tree. But the Cat keeps his side of the bargain too. He will kill mice and he will be kind to Babies when he is in the house, just as long as they do not pull his tail too hard. But when he had done that, and between times, and when the moon gets up and night comes, he is the Cat that walks by himself, and all places are alike to him. Then he goes out to the Wet Wild Woods or up the Wet Wild Trees or on the Wet Wild Roofs, waving his wild tail and walking by his wild lone.

Kipling's mastery of tone and of vision is close to absolute here, and makes us realize again how many kinds of story he abounds in, and how many perspectives he creates. Of story writers in the Twentieth century, Kipling stands just below Henry James, D. H. Lawrence, and James Joyce, but he compares very adequately with Jorge Luis Borges and Isaac Babel, as the late Irving Howe justly observed.

Rudyard Kipling

Joseph Rudyard Kipling was born December 30, 1865, in Bombay, India, where his father, John Lockwood Kipling (both went by their middle names), had been offered an artist-crafsman post at the Jeejeebhoy School of Art and Industry. Married earlier that year and recent arrivals to the subcontinent, the Kiplings were social climbers who quickly aspired to a higher position within the rigid Anglo-Indian hierarchy in which they found themselves, particularly Rudyard's mother Alice, a witty and intelligent but somewhat self-involved woman ill-suited to raising a headstrong boy. As a result, Kipling spent the majority of his early years in the company of his *ayah* (nanny) and other native servants who, by most accounts, spoiled and cultured him in equal measure.

Following Anglo-Indian custom, the Kiplings sent "Ruddy" and his younger sister "Trix" (nee Alice) back to England when they were five and three, respectively. Unconventionally, they left the children in the care of complete strangers who they found through a newspaper advertisement. The simplest and most widely attested explanation for why they would perpetrate such a Dickensian cruelty is that Ruddy had become a holy terror whose boisterous antics over previous visits had left family members indisposed to babysitting. Whatever the case, Rudyard didn't see his parents again for nearly six years. Living in "The House of Desolation," as he later called it, under the reproachful eye of a bitter woman and her much older husband was, by Rudyard's own account, an experience in abject misery, memorably depicted in the early story "Baa Baa, Black Sheep." Ruddy and Trix's only escapes were during sporadic visits to the idyllic manor of their aunt Georgie and her painter husband Edward Burne-Jones, a gathering place for pre-Raphaelite artists and other bohemian intellectuals who probably proved more receptive, at least in the short term, to Kipling's imaginative shenanigans.

In 1878, Rudyard began attending the United Services

College in Westward Ho!, North Devon, essentially a military prep school chosen by virtue of its reasonable fees and the fact that it was run by a family friend, Cornell Price. Despite (or perhaps because of) this seeming protection, Kipling suffered a fair amount of hazing from the older children (his ever-present glasses earned him the nickname of "Giglamps"), but in due course began to display his typical precociousness and a rare literary talent. Quite a few stories and poems written during this period are still extant; Alice Kipling even collected some of the latter and published them privately in India (unbeknownst to Rudyard) under the title *Schoolboy Lyrics*. Rudyard also formed a mischievous trio with two other boys. Many of their exploits later found their way into *Stalky & Co* (1899).

In 1882, on Price's recommendation and thanks to a little parental string-pulling, the sixteen-year-old Kipling left school to take a position as reporter and sub-editor for the *Civil and Military Gazette*, in Lahore, India, where his father had become principal of the Mayo School of Art and Curator of the Lahore Museum. Rudyard apparently took to the work immediately, and was often called to fill in for his chief and run the paper's entire operation during times of illness. It was during this trial by fire, no doubt, that Kipling developed the strong work ethic, embodied by so many of his characters, that fueled his prodigious literary output. Another major influence at this time was his initiation into a local Masonic lodge. With few exceptions, Kipling thereafter preferred the company of soldiers, statesmen, and other men of action to that of fellow writers and artists. He also began to incorporate themes of secret knowledge and male camaraderie into his writing. The poems and stories chronicling Anglo-Indian life that Kipling wrote (often pseudonymously) for the *CMG* and its larger sister paper, the Allahabad *Pioneer*, provided the bulk of what was collected in *Departmental Ditties* (1886) and *Plain Tales from the Hills* (1888). These, and several collections following closely on their heels, launched Kipling's career and earned him a wide readership and early fame, both in India and England.

In 1887 Kipling was promoted to the staff of the *Pioneer*, which commissioned him to write travel pieces, among other things, that sent him gallivanting across India. Two years later, wanderlust overtook him entirely and he left India in 1889 to see the world, traveling extensively throughout the Far East and America. Afterwards, Kipling settled for a time in London, extending his fame and fortune with more stories and poems as well his first novel, *The Light that Failed* (1890).

During this period Kipling also struck up a strong friendship with Wolcott Balestier, an American agent and fellow writer who was sympathetic to the many copyright abuses already inflicted on Kipling by unscrupulous American publishers. The pair collaborated on an adventure novel, *The Naulahka*, and Balestier introduced Kipling to his sister Caroline (Carrie), with whom Kipling was soon engaged. Wolcott, a victim of typhoid in 1891, did not live to see them wed or his novel in print. Rudyard and Carrie married a month later and then set sail for a honeymoon trip around the world that was cut short in Japan when Rudyard's bank collapsed and he lost over £2,000. They then settled for several years in Carrie's hometown of Brattleboro, Vermont, during which time they had two daughters (Josephine and Elsie); built a house on a plot of land purchased from Carrie's other brother Beatty; and Kipling wrote the children's classics, *The Jungle Book* and *The Second Jungle Book*, as well as many other stories and poems.

In early 1896, a quarrel with Beatty over his misappropriation of some house-building funds culminated in a physical altercation with Rudyard, who apparently backed away from the fight and then pressed charges of assault. The much-publicized row eventually forced the Kiplings to leave America for good and proved to be only the first of several successive heartbreak and tragedies. Six weeks after they returned to England, Kipling's beloved uncle Edward Burne-Jones died of a heart attack. Two years later, Trix had a nervous breakdown. The following winter the Kiplings sailed for New York with their three children (a son, John, was born in 1897) and either en route or upon arrival the entire family contracted one illness or another. Six-year-old Josephine died while Rudyard narrowly escaped a bout of double pneumonia.

That Kipling came through these dark years "a sadder and a harder man" (as his sister Trix put it nearly forty years later) is evidenced by the ever-more reactionary and imperialist sentiments he began to espouse in such verses as "White Man's Burden" and "Recessional." Nevertheless, Kipling retained some measure of his quirky ambivalence by doggedly refusing to accept multiple offers of knighthood and other state honors. He also continued to write at his usual prolific rate. From 1900 to 1906, between winters in South Africa and his now-permanent home in Sussex, Kipling published his masterwork, *Kim*, as well as *Just So Stories*, *The Five Nations*, *Traffics and Discoveries*, and *Puck of Pook's Hill*. This spate of literary successes culminated in Kipling receiving the Nobel Prize for Literature in 1907 (the first awarded to an English writer) as well as honorary degrees from Durham and Oxford.

Tragedy was not quite finished with Kipling, however. In 1915, his son John, a soldier in the Irish Guards, became missing in action at the Battle of Loos. The boy's body was never found during his father's lifetime. In response, Kipling developed duodenal ulcers that would ultimately kill him, but he also channeled his grief into two final collections of stories, *Debits and Credits* (1926) and *Limits and Renewals* (1932). Both display the reflective turn of a man searching for healing, redemption, and forgiveness. Kipling spent his last years presciently striving to convince anyone who would listen that another war with Germany was coming. He died January 18, 1936, and was buried in the Poet's Corner at Westminster Abbey. His collection of autobiographical sketches, *Something of Myself*, was published the following year.

"The Man Who Would Be King"

"The Man Who Would Be King" was originally published in 1888 in *The Phantom Rickshaw*, and was among the last stories Kipling wrote in India. Regarded by many as his most explicit allegory of colonialism, it is nonetheless an ambivalent one, using a frame story to distance both narrator and reader from the story within the story and create a kind of internal dialectic that is tailor-made for literary interpretation.

The frame story, told by an unnamed newspaperman, is comprised of five encounters with one or both of Peachey Taliaferro Carnehan and Daniel Dravot, two itinerant con men and former soldiers. In the first, the narrator meets Carnehan while traveling in an "Intermediate," or third-class, train car and the two strike up an immediate rapport based on their mutual interest in travel, adventure, and "the politics of Loaferdom, that sees things from the underside where the lath and plaster is not smoothed off." Typical of Kipling, his choice of meeting place is far from haphazard, for the narrator also functions as an intermediate, literally acting as middleman between Carnehan and Dravot, but also in the figurative sense of an intermediary between the reader and the inner narrative. Similarly, Carnehan's admission of impersonating a news correspondent in order to receive better treatment and free handouts at various stops along the railway line is meant to cue the reader to an elaborate framework of ironic doublings that supports and reinforces the story's central theme of illusion versus reality. Carnehan is a surrogate "reporter," just as the narrator is a surrogate "audience."

Before they part ways, Carnehan asks the narrator to relay a cryptic message for him to a friend (Dravot) whose path he will cross at Marwar Junction, bolstering the request by engaging the narrator in an encoded dialogue that indicates they are both Freemasons and thus bound to help one another. In the second encounter, the narrator does as he is asked, locating Dravot by his distinctive red beard. Afterwards, the narrator decides to alert the authorities about these two "loafers," rationalizing his betrayal with the conviction that he is saving them from bigger trouble. Believing the matter settled, the narrator returns to his office and his quotidian duties, "where there were no Kings and no incidents outside the daily manufacture of a newspaper."

The third encounter occurs the following June, during a "remarkably evil season" when temperatures are high and sickness running rampant. Carnehan and Dravot barge into the narrator's office late one night and demand a "favour" from him to make up for his earlier betrayal. They want information on "Kafiristan," a vast and (then) uncharted region north of the imperial frontier that includes parts of modern-day Pakistan and Afghanistan that they plan to conquer by (following England's precedent in India) pitting local tribes against one another, after which they "will subvert that King and seize his Throne and establish a Dy-nasty." Justifiably dubious, the narrator nonetheless provides them with maps and books. The adventurers, in turn, show the narrator their "Contrack" which essentially says they will stick by one another, swear off liquor and women, and "settle this matter together, i.e. to be Kings of Kafiristan."

The fourth encounter occurs the following morning, when the narrator goes down to the Serai to say goodbye to the adventurers. Dravot and Carnehan have disguised themselves as a mad priest and his servant, respectively, and the narrator initially fails to recognize them. This is another example of Kipling using a seemingly minor event to convey several things at once. First, in their ability to "fool" the cynical narrator, Dravot and Carnehan display an unprecedented level of cunning and aptitude, prepping both narrator and reader for the suspension of disbelief required to swallow Carnehan's outrageous tale. This effect is augmented by the revelation that they have acquired 20 Martini rifles—capable weapons for capable men. Secondly, the emphasis on recognition—or the (in)ability to determine real from false, truth from fiction— further develops Kipling's theme. Lastly, in another ironic doubling, Dravot's false madness foreshadows Carnehan's actual madness at story's end.

A couple years pass before the fifth and final encounter with Carnehan, when the inner story is finally told. The physical changes wrought by his ordeal have transformed the big man into a "rag-wrapped, whining cripple" and once again the narrator does not recognize him. Nevertheless, he is intrigued enough to ply the man with whiskey and listen to his tale.

From the outset Carnehan's faculties are suspect. He speaks of mountains fighting "like wild goats" and refers to himself in the third person. But after relating their first encounter with the natives, who turn out to be fair-haired descendants of Alexander the Great's army, his narration gradually becomes more coherent. Everything went according to plan, more or less, and with the aid of their long-range rifles, army training, a smattering of diplomacy and improvised ritual, they quickly establish control over the less sophisticated Kafirs. Dravot, being the natural charismatic of two, takes on the role of king and Carnehan becomes commander-in-chief. Within a few months they have conquered the entire area. But their real apotheosis occurs when a chief gives Dravot a secret Masonic handshake of the Second Degree and Dravot trumps him with one of the Third. Dravot sets about establishing a new lodge, with himself as Grand Master of course, and when the "Master's Mark" Dravot has directed be put on his new-made apron matches one carved on the underside of a temple stone, his dominion is assured.

Unsurprisingly, all that power overwhelms Dravot's better judgment and he decides to break his contract with Carnehan (and the unwritten rules of godhood) by taking a native for a wife. Frightened, the chosen woman bites Dravot's lip, draws blood, and exposes him as a mortal. General mutiny erupts, with the natives howling "Not a God nor a Devil but only a man!" Dravot, Carnehan, and a few trusted men flee but they are quickly overtaken. Dravot heroically assumes sole responsibility in the hopes of saving Carnehan (and thus fulfilling some measure of his claims to kingliness) and heads out onto a rope bridge over a ravine. The natives cut the bridge and Dravot falls to his death. For his part, Carnehan is crucified between two pine trees. When he miraculously survives, the natives take him down and send him back to India, where he finds the narrator and recounts the tale.

The frame story ends with the narrator discovering Carnehan crawling by the roadside later that same day and taking him to the local mission, which then has him committed to an asylum. Seeking him out two days later, the narrator finds Carnehan has died of sunstroke. Again Kipling is doubling back; just as Carnehan's faux madness has become manifestly real, so too has the sunstroke suggested by the narrator when Dravot and Carnehan first proposed their wild plan. Dravot's severed head is just one more girder in the same ironic framework; the would-be king has quite literally lost his mind. But just in case Carnehan's schizophrenic delivery and the general outrageousness of the inner narrative aren't enough, Kipling is sure to point out that Dravot's head (and the gold crown proving his kinghood) has disappeared: "and there the matter rests."

Of course, the "the matter" is anything but settled and therein lies the genius of the story. By explicitly allegorizing the colonial enterprise, by provoking the reader with a series of ironic doublings that reflect and refract the theme of illusion versus reality, but most of all by embedding a morally and factually questionable adventure yarn inside a cynical narrative framework, Kipling is practically ensuring that the tale will be read and questioned on several levels at once.

"The Man Who Would Be King"

Peachey Taliaferro Carnehan is the more pragmatic of the two adventurers and the one who survives the ordeal just long enough to relate the story to the narrator. Though his schizophrenic delivery puts his credibility in doubt, the gold crown on Dravot's severed head corroborates some of his claims.

Daniel Dravot is the charismatic but foolhardy would-be king who manages (if we can believe Peachey's story) to conquer an entire region with no more than twenty rifles, a little diplomacy, good luck, and some knowledge of Masonic ritual. His hubristic decision to take a native woman for a wife leads to his downfall and death, but his actions in death recover some measure of nobility.

The Unnamed Narrator is a newspaperman who provides the outer frame and relaying mechanism for the inner narrative. His ironic, cynical tone and vocational concern with everyday affairs is in direct contrast to the larger-than-life personalities and imperialist ambitions of Carnehan and Dravot, yet his identification with them renders him an unreliable witness as well.

Billy Fish is a priest/chief and closest ally of Carnehan and Dravot among the natives of Kafiristan, so-named for his resemblance to a fellow who did railway construction with them "in the old days." His awareness of their charade, and the savvy he displays in the face of it, lends some credibility to Carnehan's depiction of the otherwise gullible Kafirs.

"The Man Who Would Be King"

PAUL FUSSELL ON THE STORY'S MASONIC ALLUSIONS

[Paul Fussell is the Donald T. Regan Professor Emeritus of English Literature at the University of Pennsylvania. Among many other works, he is the author of *The Great War and Modern Memory* (1975), which won him the National Book Award and the National Book Critics Circle Award. In the following extract, Fussell illuminates the story's many Masonic references.]

Three years before "The Man Who Would Be King" appeared (1888), Kipling had become a Freemason, joining the Lodge "Hope and Perseverance, No. 789, E. C." at Lahore.[8] The story abounds with Masonic references and jokes, and these lend depth and quality to both the serious theme and the playful, ironic treatment. The epigraph, "Brother to a Prince and fellow to a beggar if he be found worthy," stems from Masonic tradition and appears in a different form in Kipling's poem "'Banquet Night,'" written for a Masonic banquet:

> ... once, in so often the messenger brings
> Solomon's mandate: "Forget these things!
> Brother to Beggars and Fellow to Kings,
> Companion of Princes—forget these things!"

"These things" are differences of origin and profession which separate Freemasons outside the lodge but which they are charged to forget while attending Masonic functions.[9] The connection of Freemasonry with the idea of natural kingship is also suggested in Kipling's poem "The Palace," which begins,

> When I was a King and a Mason.

The story clearly issues from a young mind excited by Masonic symbolism and Masonic ethical precepts, and, in a sense, the ethical system of the story could be said to be Masonic. Dravot and Carnahan, with their adherence to ideals of order and, regularity and in their acts of sacrifice and fidelity at the end of the story, behave as if conscious of Masonic obligations. From the beginning of his career to the end, Kipling found himself at all times interested in and sometimes obsessed by the subject of kingship, and similar Masonic attitudes towards the question of "real" vs. "actual" kings are expressed in poems like "What the People Said" and "A Servant When He Reigneth."

British Freemasonry has been fond of the theme of kingship since the appearance of James Anderson's *The Constitutions of the Free-Masons* in 1723. In this work, which has become one of the ritual classics of Freemasonry, Anderson stresses the antiquity and dignity of the craft by pointing to all the kings who have been Freemasons, beginning with Noah, Moses, and Solomon (the description of whose temple, in *I Kings*, 5–8, is the source of much Masonic symbolism) and continuing up through Western history to European Renaissance and Enlightenment monarchs. The race of Noah, Anderson tells us, "upon their Dispersion carry'd the mighty Knowledge [of Freemasonry] with them into distant Parts, where they found the good use of it in the Settlement of KINGDOMS, COMMONWEALTHS, and DYNASTIES."[10] He asserts that "the ISRAELITES ... were a whole Kingdom of MASONS, well instructed, under the Conduct of their GRAND MASTER MOSES, who often marshall'd them into a regular and GENERAL LODGE, while in the Wilderness, and gave them wise CHARGES, ORDERS, &c...."[11] And "the WISE KING SOLOMON was GRAND MASTER of the LODGE: at JERUSALEM...."[12] The similarity of these notions to the ideas according to which Dravot and Carnahan conduct themselves in Kafiristan is not, one may suppose, coincidental. It would appear that Kipling, as a young and enthusiastic Mason, studied *The Constitutions* diligently (new Masons are usually given a copy), was amused by Anderson's attribution of Masonic knowledge and virtues to the Hebraic kings, and found himself unable to resist writing an esoteric and rococo Masonic story in which two outcasts unconsciously burlesque the traditional early history of Freemasonry. Although Kipling's acquaintance with *The Constitutions* undoubtedly stimulated his search for Biblical parallels, his acquaintance with the Bible was so thorough that the Biblical background would probably appear in the story even if he had never heard of Anderson.

The presence of this Masonic joke in an early story by one who was to be taxed with the crudest kind of jingo imperialism is not without interest, for Freemasonry is essentially an Anglo-Saxon institution, and its spread to India and the East is an apt symbol of the triumph there of British institutions during the eighteenth and nineteenth centuries. The first formal Grand Lodge of Masons was organized in London in 1717, and the movement, after spreading to Scotland and Ireland, gradually extended to the continent, to the Mediterranean, and so into India and the Fast, carrying with it its freight of fundamentally Deistic and Enlightenment ideas: its emphasis on universal brotherhood; its search for the common element in mankind; its disinclination to quarrel over politics and religion; and its classical emphasis on self-mastery, order, and restraint.[13] Kipling was influenced not only by the symbolism and ethics of Freemasonry but also by the paradigm of Anglo-Saxon powers of expansion and penetration which the rapid growth of the movement exhibited. The importance of Freemasonry to Kipling may be appreciated when we see him using the swastika on the fly-leaves and title-page versos of his books: the swastika, especially when enclosed in a circle, is an important Masonic mark.

The most interesting Masonic element in "The Man Who Would Be King," however, is the symbolism of the crucifixion of Peachey. J. S. M. Ward has said that "in modern Freemasonry we may have an intellectualised survival of the cult of the Dying God and of the Fertility rites...."[14] The symbolism of many of the higher degrees of the craft involves emblems of rebirth derived, ultimately, from the fertility cults of the Mediterranean area,[15] and a whole school of Masonic "scholarship" has devoted itself to investigating the anthropological origins of present-day Masonic symbolism. It seems not unlikely that Kipling, in his first flush of Masonic excitement, may have become interested in the writings of this school, and that the symbolism of Peachey's crucifixion owes as much to Masonic as it does to Christian tradition. At least we can say that the presence of this crucifixion in a story so packed with Masonic materials suggests that this further bit of half-whimsical, half-sober symbolism derives from the same source.

NOTES

8. Carrington, pp. 54–55.

9. See Kipling's poem "The Mother-Lodge," in which a sort of Carnahan persona speaks in dialect:

> Outside—"Sergeant! Sir! Salute! Salaam!"
> Inside—"Brother," an' it doesn't do no 'arm.
> We met upon the Level an' we parted on the Square,
> An' I was Junior Deacon in my Mother-Lodge out there!

This poem seems to embody exactly Kipling's youthful excitement over the potential of Freemasonry for breaking down caste and racial barriers in India.

10. *The Constitutions of the Free-Masons. Containing the History, Charges, Regulations, &c. of that most Ancient and Right Worshipful Fraternity* (London, 1723), p. 4.

11. *Ibid.*, pp. 8–9.

12. *Ibid.*, p. 14.

13. It may be noted that, although the relationship between Freemasonry and eighteenth century British literary and intellectual history is a most promising area for research, it has hardly been touched.

14. "Freemasonry,", *Encyclopedia Britannica* (Chicago, 1953).

15. See Ward, *Freemasonry and the Ancient Gods.*

> —Paul Fussell, "Irony, Freemasonry, and Humane Ethics in Kipling's 'The Man Who Would Be King.'" *Journal of English Literary History* 25 (1958): pp. 216–33.

LOUIS L. CORNELL ON THE MEANING OF DRAVOT AND CARNEHAN'S FAILURE

[Louis L. Cornell is the editor of *The Man Who Would Be King and Other Stories* and author of *Kipling in India*, a focused look at Kipling's literary apprenticeship. In this extract from the latter, Cornell examines the allegorical implications of Dravot and Carnehan's downfall.]

'The Man Who Would Be King', the best of the stories Kipling wrote in India, must conclude any study of his apprenticeship, not only because of its brilliance, but because in a sense it embodies and sums up Kipling's attitude to India and the role of the British in the land they had conquered. The story is susceptible of innumerable interpretations: in its mysterious way it is concerned with issues larger than the adventures of a pair of English ne'er-do-wells in the unexplored hills of Kafiristan.[1] Nevertheless, the form of the tale is straightforward. Dravot and Carnehan are tragic figures, conquerors who, like Tamburlaine, conceive the ambition of becoming emperors. They are above the common run of mankind; they are as strong and vigorous as Mulvaney, as subtle at disguise as Strickland, as worldly and cynical as McIntosh Jellaludin. With courage and luck they pile success upon success until they become gods in the eyes of their primitive subjects. But in the end they violate the conditions of their success. Dravot overreaches himself in wanting to take a wife from among their subjects, and his failure of judgment causes him to pull down upon his own head the frail structure his courage and ambition have reared.

Like 'A Wayside Comedy', 'The Man Who Would Be King' is peculiarly Indian in the moral experiment to which its heroes are subjected. 'A Wayside Comedy', however, displays Anglo-Indians in a state of paralysis. Isolated in the remote valley of Kashima, the heirs of the conquerors are unable to enjoy the fruits of conquest. They are a far-flung patrol of an army of occupation, but they lack the inner strength to survive the rigours of such a calling; India is too much for them. In a sense, 'The Man Who Would Be King' looks back to an earlier generation, a generation less troubled by boredom, isolation, and responsibility. Dravot and Carnehan recapitulate the British conquest.[2] Like Clive and the great generals who followed him, they prove that a disciplined native army, provided with effective weapons, is a match for a much larger force of untrained tribesmen. Like the great Anglo-Indian administrators, they find the land divided by petty rulers: they put an end to internecine war, establish the pax Britannica, and win the support of tribesmen who prefer subjection to anarchy. Even their motives show the odd mixture of patriotism and personal ambition that characterized the men who conquered the world for England: '"... we'd be an Empire. When everything was shipshape, I'd hand over the crown—this crown I'm wearing now—to Queen Victoria on my knees, and she'd say: 'Rise up, Sir Daniel Dravot.'"'

Why, then, does this simulacrum of the Indian Empire fall and crush its makers? The meaning of Dravot's and Carnehan's failure is complex. On the one hand, they have effected their conquest under false pretences. They have concealed from their people the real significance of the Masonic Mark; '"'Only the Gods know that,'"' says Billy Fish; '"'We thought you were men till you showed the Sign of the Master.'"' In Kipling's stories deceit is often a risky business: the truth that underlies situations and men has a powerful tendency to manifest itself. Kafiristan, like India, is a place of extremes; circumstances corrode and destroy false appearances. On the other hand, Dravot and Carnehan succeed as gods and fail only when their manhood is revealed. One of the many ironies of the story is provided by Carnehan's perpetual awareness of his rough-and-tumble background, his continual reduction of their royal acts to the terms he best understands. And so, when Dravot proposes to take a wife—'"'A Queen out of the strongest tribe, that'll make them your blood-brothers, and that'll lie by your side and tell you all the people thinks about you and their own affairs'"'—Carnehan can see it only in terms of a casual liaison with a native girl: '"'Do you remember that Bengali woman I kept at Mogul Serai when I was a platelayer?' says I. 'A fat lot o' good she was to me.'"' Dravot is justifiably angered by the comparison; and yet Peachey is not entirely wrong about Dravot's motives: rather, he is oversimplifying them. Dravot's desire for a queen is more than lust and more than political strategy; in a sense, it is one of those gestures towards a real contact with the conquered land that occur in Plain Tales and always come to nothing. Like the British in India, Dravot and Carnehan can move just so far in the direction of acclimatizing themselves to Kafiristan before they are forcibly reminded that an immense gulf lies between them and their subjects. Reducing the problem to his own simple terms, Carnehan sums it up thus: '"There's no accounting for natives. This business is our 'Fifty-Seven.'"' It is appropriate that Dravot, the unsuccessful builder of a bridge between races, should die as he does, hurled into a chasm from a broken bridge, a bridge that has been destroyed by the tribesmen he has tried to civilize and enlighten.

NOTES

1. The most complex and suggestive analysis of the story is by Paul Fussell, Jr.: 'Irony, Freemasonry, and Humane Ethics in Kipling's "The Man Who Would Be King"', *ELH*, xxv (1958), 216–33. Prof. Fussell elucidates many of Kipling's Biblical and Masonic allusions and does a thorough and illuminating job of close reading. He is not concerned with the social and historical backgrounds that seem to me of importance to a full understanding of the story.

2. The view of 'The Man Who Would Be King' as a myth of imperialism was brought forward many years ago by Eugène Marie Melchior, Vicomte de Vogüé, 'Les Pères de l'impérialisme anglais', in *Pages d'histoire* (Paris, 1902), pp. 121–34. The references in the story to Rajah Brooke of Sarawak make it plain that Kipling also had recent events in mind and that Dravot and Carnehan are explicitly intended to represent a phase of British imperialism. In this connection, it should be noted that the crucifixion of Carnehan, whatever its symbolic role in the story, probably first made contemporary readers think of the rumours that British captives were being crucified by the Burmese in the wars of the late eighties.

—Louis L. Cornell, *Kipling in India* (New York: St. Martin's Press, 1966): pp. 161–165.

THOMAS A. SHIPPEY AND MICHAEL SHORT ON SYNTAX AND TECHNIQUE

[Thomas A. Shippey is Chair of the Humanities Department at Saint Louis University and the author of numerous works on medieval literature, including *J.R.R. Tolkien: Author of the Century* and *Beowulf*. Michael Short is a Professor of Language and Literature at Lancaster University (UK), the author of *Exploring the Language of Poems, Plays and Prose*, and co-author of *Style in Fiction*. In the following short excerpt from their masterful exegesis of the story's technique, Shippey and Short identify and interpret the linguistic abnormalities in Carnehan's narrative.]

The technical question of greatest interest [regarding "The Man Who Would Be King"] must be: "how can Kipling create and maintain an idiosyncratic style which has to convey impressions of a near-incredible world without at the same time alienating his readers?" The answers are, for 1888, unexpectedly subtle linguistically. They can be reached most easily by comparing Carnehan's speech with the skilful, reasonable, but no longer entirely self-confident style of the 'I' narrator explaining what happens in the "frames."

One obvious point must be made first. Carnehan—who has after all been crucified—is clearly mad. At the start of his narrative he asks the "I" narrator to keep looking him in the eyes "'or maybe my words will all go to pieces.'" Five times after this the current of his speech is broken by some digression or interjection, as he has to be called back to his subject; nevertheless, these reminders of insanity gradually become less obtrusive, and the story gathers pace and clarity. However, as he reaches the climax—Dravot's death and his own crucifixion— Carnehan begins to wander again. He goes back to speaking of himself in the third person; he reverts to a beggar's servility; he confuses himself and Dravot:

> "But Peachey, Peachey Taliaferro, I tell you, Sir, in confidence as betwixt two friends, he lost his head, Sir. No, he didn't, neither. The King lost his head, so he did, all along o' one of those cunning rope-bridges. Kindly let me have the paper-cutter, Sir. It tilted this way...."

In a way, this flight from reality only confirms that some traumatic event has in fact occurred; but certainty as to what would be inappropriate. It is at this blend of madness and sense, realism and mystery, that Kipling is aiming.

Probably the first distinguishing mark of the monologue is its lack of normal temporal or causative sequence. After the narrator's second interruption, as Carnehan starts to tell of the entry into Kafiristan, we are given a sample of his wandering mind:

> "And then there camels were no use, and Peachey said to Dravot—'For the Lord's sake let's get out of this before our heads are chopped off,' and with that they killed the camels all among the mountains, not having anything in particular to eat, but first they took off the boxes with the guns and ammunition, till two men came along driving four mules."

In this sentence the last conjunction "till" is not accompanied by the usual lexical items of duration (*c.f.* "they sat there till ..."? "they waited till ..."?); killing the camels and taking off their loads are given in the wrong order; "all among the mountains" is pleonastic; and the threat of decapitation seems to come from nowhere and lead to nothing. Yet the outline of a desperate situation is dimly visible, while the quotation, the extra details, and the backtracking suggest also a struggle for exactness on Peachey's part. His lame and abrupt conjunctions "and then ... and ... and with that ... but first" further imply events too powerful and immediate for the speaker to control them. Similar vagaries appear repeatedly near this place. A few lines before Carnehan has explained that the country was too mountainous for camels, with curious redundancy: "'That was in a most mountaineous country, and our camels couldn't go along any more because of the mountains.'" A little later he repeats himself more rhetorically: "'The country was mountaineous and the mules were most contrary and the inhabitants was dispersed and solitary.'" Partly the effect is comic, as "high-style" vocabulary ("most contrary ... inhabitants ... solitary") clashes with "low-style" grammar ("inhabitants was"); but also the repetitiousness, the drift of irrelevance, and the very positive nature of Peachey's assertions, give a sense of curious, almost monotonous immediacy to the journey. It is as if the narrator can remember what has happened, but has little idea of which events are more important than others; we are made aware of the process of recall as much as its results.

That this sensation was produced deliberately is proved by

Kipling's highlighting of Peachey's syntactic meanderings through contrast with the very careful and lucid interjections of the editor-narrator.

> "Take some more whisky," I said very slowly, "What did you and Daniel Dravot do *when* the camels could go no farther *because* of the rough roads *that* led into Kafiristan?" ... He paused for a moment, *while* I asked him *if* he could remember the nature of the country *through which* he had journeyed. [The words which mark the relations between grammatical units, conjunctions and relative pronouns. have been italicized]

The contrast points out Peachey's madness; but it shows also that his manner of speech is consistent even in its abnormality. The opposition of official and "Loafer," present from the first scene of the "frames," is mirrored here by different linguistic habits, the one controlled, organizing, "editing," the other seeming to present raw experience in a manner unacceptable to many, but nevertheless not to be summarily dismissed as mere imagination.

This comparative lack of connections does not deny a certain rhetorical and even poetic impulse in Peachey. We have seen this already in his near recitative "all among the mountains." There are flashes of wit, often, in the conversations he reports, as when Dravot kills a man for his mules:

> "Dravot up and dances in front of them, singing—'Sell me four mules.' Says the first man—'If you are rich enough to buy you are rich enough to rob'; but before ever he could put his hand to his knife, Dravot breaks his neck over his knee ..."

There is a certain rhythmic heightening in the alliterative parallels of "hand ... knife ... neck ... knee," and also in the neat concealed antithesis of "rich enough to buy ... rich enough to rob," where the first infinitive is of course active in sense ("to buy from us"), the second passive ("to be robbed by us"). A certain power of this kind—not often present in the narrator's drier style—helps to make the monologue more impressive in a disorderly way; with another device (rather rare in modern standard English) Kipling manages to make such impressiveness more prominent, and also to connect it increasingly with the dominant but unlucky figure of Dravot.

This device is known to linguists as the use of "marked theme."[9] Most English declarative sentences, in a language now uninflected, follow very strictly the order Subject–Verb–Object, with only limited freedom as to where to put adverbial and connective elements. Repeatedly Peachey breaks these rules of normal word-order, from his first appearance in the narrator's office in scene E: "'I've come back,' he repeated; "'and I was the King of Kafiristan—me and Dravot—*crowned Kings* we was! *In this office* we settled it ...'" (In this quotation, and subsequently, "marked theme" has been italicized; it is worth noting that on all but two occasions of those cited, it is the Object or Complement of the sentence which has been moved to the front—the most unusual and hence most marked form of "marked theme.") At this point, the breaches of normal word-order perhaps seem only a slightly vulgar form of emphasis, connected with Peachey's false concords ("we was"). But as the monologue continues these breaches occur in increasingly grave contexts, and begin to take on an alternative range of suggestions—not vulgar and colloquial, but archaic and, especially, Biblical.[10] In these circumstances "marked theme" is associated in particular with Dravot, who as the story continues becomes more and more the king and the rash, ruling spirit, with Peachey acting as his restraint and acolyte. Early on, Peachey distinguishes between them: "'I wasn't King,'" said Carnehan. "'Dravot he was the King and *a handsome man* he looked with the gold crown on his head and all.'" Later, as Dravot returns from his first triumphal expedition, he boasts to Peachey of the riches of their dominion: "'*Gold* I've seen, and *turquoise* I've kicked out of the cliffs, and there's garnets in the sands of the river....'" He explains also that the Kafirs have a rudimentary Masonic organization, and that this is to be their means of control: "'*A God and a Grand-Master of the Craft* am I, and *a Lodge in the Third Degree*—I will open....'"

Peachey protests that this is illegal, but is overborne: "'I've forty chiefs at my heel, and *passed and raised according to their merits* they shall be.'" This imperative and overbearing streak reappears in Dravot, to be expressed in similar fashion every time he makes a major error. Meddling with the Masonic organisation is one. Breaking the "Contrack" by taking a wife is the next, again over Peachey's appeals: "'These women are whiter than you or me, and *a Queen* I will have for the winter months.'" And when the "Queen" exposes Dravot's humanity (by biting him) and the Kafirs rebel, we see the megalomania persisting in Dravot in spite of his failure: "'*An Emperor* am I,'" says Daniel, "'and *next Year* I shall be a Knight of the Queen.'"

These instances are of course dispersed through a fairly long story (which however contains other examples). But the sensitivity of any native speaker to such abnormalities is very high;[11] they contribute a tone, even if they are never analyzed grammatically or consciously. The utility of "marked theme" for Kipling lies largely in its potential ambiguity. The device often suggests will-power and imperiousness in Dravot; it can also be just faintly comic. As he ruminates on his Kingdom's potential, Dravot considers bringing in other Englishmen as deputies: "'There's Mackray, Sergeant-pensioner at Segowli—*many's the good dinner* he's given me, and his wife a pair of trousers.'" The second-hand trousers co-exist with the golden crown, and Dravot notices no incongruity. Moreover, the incongruity which the reader notices does not entirely detract from the narrative. Like Peachey's rambling style, it even contains a hint of verisimilitude; for just as the "Loafer" in Dravot emerges in the middle of his Kingship, so even in their most obvious scenes of "Loaferdom" Carnehan and Dravot show flashes of regal self-assurance—as we have seen, just enough to shake the "I" narrator's scepticism at two or three moments. The linguistic habits associated with Dravot continue the work of the "frames"; they give strong suggestions of discrepant worlds co-existing, but forbid any final resolution.

There should be no doubt that Kipling, with his notorious sensitivity to language, knew in these cases exactly what he was doing.

9. For discussion of "marked theme," see M. A. K. Halliday, "Notes on Transitivity and Theme in English, Part 2," *Journal of Linguistics* 3 (1967), 199–244, and also J. M. Sinclair, *A Course in Spoken English: Grammar*, Ch. 2, section 12, to be published in 1972 by Oxford University Press.

10. No statistics on this subject exist. There are, for instance, seven examples of "marked theme" in the first chapter of *Genesis* (Authorised Version).

11. This is especially true of "Object Theme," as in normal English the post-verbal position is one of the main features allowing one to recognize what the object is.

—Thomas A. Shippey and Michael Short, "Framing and Distancing in Kipling's 'The Man Who Would Be King'." *The Journal of Narrative Technique* 2, no. 2 (May 1972): pp. 79–82.

PHILLIP MALLETT ON THE STORY'S MORAL AMBIVALENCE

[Phillip Mallett is a Senior Lecturer in English at the University of St. Andrews. He is the author and/or editor of several books on Thomas Hardy and editor of Kipling's *Limits and Renewals* (1987). Mallett plumbs the story's moral murkiness in the following extract, taken from his contribution to a collection of essays he also edited.]

'The Man Who Would Be King' (*Wee Willie Winkie*, 1888) is an earlier story, one of the last pieces Kipling wrote before leaving India.[5] Two men, describing themselves to the newspaperman who is the narrator as 'loafers', set off to exploit their military skill, and their twenty Martini rifles, in Kafiristan, intending to become kings and to make their fortunes. Their weapons and expertise help them on the way to success, and the natives are half-persuaded by their astonishing powers of killing at a distance to accept them as gods, but their real triumph comes when their knowledge, as freemasons, of hidden and ancient symbols known only to a very few priests seems to confirm their divine status. This, however, also proves their undoing. Dravot, the more dominant of the two, finding himself burdened by a growing sense of the responsibilities of kingship, decides to take a wife; terrified of a match with a god the girl bites him, and when he bleeds the imposture is revealed. Dravot is killed, but his companion Carnehan survives crucifixion just long enough to return to tell their tale to the newspaperman.

The hoax here is the pretence that the two men are gods, descendants of Alexander the Great. That white men who find themselves among non-whites will naturally rise to a position of authority is more or less a reflex response among white writers, from Defoe's *Robinson Crusoe* to John Boorman's film *The Emerald Forest*, and the idea of the white incomer being taken for god is at least as old as Shakespeare's *The Tempest*.[6] Typically, Kipling draws the reader's attention to these assumptions, but then, having flaunted them, declines to register any anxiety about them. Kipling allows the reader to recognise that Dravot cannot live up to the expectations created by his claim to a godlike status, but does not go on to suggest that such claims are inherently fraudulent, that the burden the white man has seen as his by right is too heavy to be carried. The implicit charge against Dravot is not that he made the claim, but that he dropped it: that, because his was a kind of *lumpen* version of the grander British imperial posture, he so far forgot himself as to marry a native, and so admit his kinship with his subjects. Dravot's error is strategic rather than moral; he gives the game away before it has been made safe (a point Carnehan tries unsuccessfully to impress upon him).

Kipling's decision to set the main story within the 'frame' of the newspaperman's encounter with the two men, first on the railway and then later in his office, serves to suggest another possible relation between their story and the larger story of British imperialism: that they may be seen as commenting on the reality underlying the fine phrases of British policy in their open desire for 'loot'. Both Carnehan and the narrator acknowledge themselves as 'loafers' and talk together 'the politics of Loaferdom', characterised by its tendency to see things 'from the underside where the lath and plaster is not smoothed off' (p. 218), and even when the narrator returns to his office and is become 'respectable', this sense of a view from the underside continues (p. 223). Anglo-India waiting for its newspaper is mocked and discredited by the narrator's sardonic account of applicants to his office—missionaries wanting to abuse other missionaries, old soldiers angry at being passed over, ladies expecting 'a hundred lady's cards printed *at once*, please' (p. 224)—and so too is the world outside, as the newspaper waits for news of a king or a courtier or a courtesan or a constitution, as if none of these really mattered. The scene is repeated later, to reinforce the sense that these are things which really don't deserve the attention customarily accorded them, and in any event the overwhelming heat (marvellously evoked in this story) saps the significance from all experience. The 'wheel of the world' swings round, but without real meaning (p. 236).

This loafer's view, then, might be expected to see, ironically and subversively, through fine phrases to a brute reality—through ideas of duty, for example, to the reality of the 'loot' beneath. Dravot and Carnehan leave India because they feel it is 'not big enough' for them: 'The country isn't half worked out because they that govern it won't let you touch it' (p. 228). They, the loafers, see that this is timidity, not a sense of responsibility, just as they see the brutality in the Native States which the administration has no need to face directly. But as Carnehan tells his story, the narrator makes no moralising comment, but listens only, and in the process the loafer's view is dropped. Dravot is seen only as he appears to Carnehan, in terms of his personality, and the only moral relation in which he stands is his relation to Carnehan, his friend and his fellow in their enterprise. Carnehan sees their hoax in entirely pragmatic terms; it works, but it is dangerous (but so too is the blackmail he had been planning against the Degumber Rajah as the story began), and they should secure their position before taking any further risks. And since Dravot's only moral relation is with his friend, he can atone for his flaws by admitting them and magnanimously offering to die alone. At the same time we are invited to share Carnehan's view of Dravot's ambitions to be a king: to make 'a damned fine Nation' of his subjects, whom he sees as all but English (p. 249). Dravot's dreams of personal glory (he expects what Rajah Brooke indeed got, a KCB) seem heroic rather than deluded to

Carnehan, and the narrator offers no reason to dissent.[7] In learning that he wants to 'make' a nation, Dravot has himself been 'made'; as compared with those kings of whom news was awaited in the office, interchangeable as they were with courtiers and courtesans, Dravot is real and charged with significance, as his fidelity to Carnehan attests. His death is not a punishment for his hoax, an index of its wrongness, but a further vindication of his moral stature. Blackmailers in the Native States die with suddenness, kings die with irritating dilatoriness when newspapers await the news; Dravot dies with heroic dignity.

By suppressing the loafer views initially shared by both Carnehan and the narrator, Kipling suppresses the possibility that the two adventurers represent a view from the underside of the imperial venture. We are given instead a quasi-tragic story, where Dravot is not condemned for his readiness to lie, or his desire for personal aggrandisement—indeed, this last becomes his virtue, his capacity for big dreams showing him capable of becoming a big man—but admired for the moral growth which has made him, if only briefly, a 'real' king; we are not asked to condemn him for his ambition, but to applaud him. This is one effect of the hymn sung near the end of the story by the now deranged Carnehan:

> The Son of God goes forth to war,
>   A kingly crown to gain;
> His blood-red banner streams afar!
>   Who follows in his train? (p. 265)

The answer, of course, is that Carnehan does, a disciple bearing the stigmata of his crucifixion, helped on his long journey by the voice of his dead friend. Dravot is both a real king, and (virtually) a real god.[8]

NOTES

5. Page references are to this story in the Sussex Edition.

6. Hugh Ridley, *Images of Imperial Rule* (London, 1983) pp. 1–8; Martin Green, *Dreams of Adventure, Deeds of Empire* (London, 1980) pp. 80–1.

7. James Brooke (1803–68) helped put down a rebellion in Sarawak, then

subject to the Malay Sultan of Brunei, and was installed as Rajah in 1842. He was made a KCB in 1848.

8. Louis Cornell describes Dravot and Carnehan as 'tragic figures', who attempt in vain to establish the 'pax Britannica', in his *Kipling in India* (London, 1966) pp. 162–3. See also Paul Fussell, 'Irony, Freemasonry, and Humane Ethics in Kipling's "The Man Who Would Be King"', *ELH*, vol. 25 (1958) pp. 216–33.

> —Phillip Mallett, "Kipling and the Hoax." *Kipling Considered* (New York: St. Martin's Press, 1989): pp. 102–105.

ZOHREH T. SULLIVAN ON DUALITY AND THE DIVIDED WORLD OF THE STORY

[Zohreh T. Sullivan is a Professor of English at the University of Illinois and editor of the forthcoming Norton Critical Edition of *Kim*. In this extract from her book on Kipling's imperialist fictions, Sullivan discusses the dialectical relationship between the frame story and the inner narrative.]

"The Man Who Would Be King" is Kipling's most powerful allegory of empire and kingship, a story of control, desire and subversion, of authority and its discontents, and of the "worst muckers" as world makers and destroyers. A small compendium of his most characteristic concerns, it is enclosed in one of his more elaborate frames that invites the reader to read the lurid embedded tale in its dialectical relationship to the oblique and strange matrix that contains it. The incident chosen for retelling is, as always, a source of displaced personal and political anxiety for the narrator who assumes a stance at once invulnerable, distant and ironic, but whose rhetoric inadvertently reveals his vulnerability and collusion.

The bare outline suggests a cautionary colonialist allegory about two daring, swashbuckling adventurers who, finding India too confining for their grandiose ambitions, decide to travel to remote, icy, and forbidden Kafiristan in order to become kings. Dravot's and Carnehan's conquest of Kafiristan, accomplished with twenty Martini rifles, a knowledge of British military drill, and a mystique of divine right based on a garbled, half-forgotten version of Masonic ritual, sounds remarkably like a seedy version of the British Raj. That their downfall is provoked by Dravot's hubris encourages us to read the story as a treatment, in schoolboy-thriller form, of Kipling's recurrent "Recessional" theme: England can retain its divinely given right to rule only so long as it retains moral superiority, a "humble and a contrite heart." The partiality of such a reading is demonstrated by the fact that it omits the most important character in the story—the narrator—who compels us to reread its meaning through the complex negotiation between the embedded adventure and the frame. The disturbance in this narrative is created by the collision between its central romantic myth and its distancing realistic, ironic frame whose narrator tempers his dispassionate perceptions of the adventurers with an elegiac and religious sentimentality. The narrator's stance relativizes his relationship to the embedded tale, distances itself from the quest of the adventurers, yet appears incapable of detaching itself from collusion in its implications. That ambivalence, so typical of Kipling, exteriorizes cultural and historical conflicts between the desire to colonize, connect and possess (country and woman) and the warning against such desire, between the glorification of imperial adventure and the cynical debunking of its origins in greed, self-aggrandizement, and childlike games of power.

Typical of Kipling's narrative strategy, the world of "The Man Who Would Be King" is radically divided. Although the initial and fundamental opposition between "Man" and "King," between the human and his politically symbolic function, is announced in the title, the larger opposition in the story is between the world of the narrator—realistic, seasoned, ironic— and that of the adventurers—romantic, flamboyant, and "mad." The duality makes some parts of the story more dreamlike than others, as if the narrator were the waking self and the embedded tale a dream, a journey into archaic fantasies charged with desire, romance and unreality. The denied and forbidden aspects of character not accessible but desired by the narrator find expression in the daring of the two bombastic and misguided adventurers whom he glorifies and exoticizes by myth and romance. If this structure, however, would seem to imply a liberating confrontation with the repressed leading to a cathartic resolution of contradiction, the story never realizes that promise. By enveloping the tale in romantic religiosity, Biblical language and the mythology of Freemasonry, Kipling seems to evade and transcend the social and political. Analogously, he displaces the problem of invasion, lawlessness and power in the story away from its historical immediacy to the personal; yet he represents that displacement in terms of the overdetermined contradictions of imperial mythology. By displacing the reader's attention from history onto the individual act in order to "manage" and defuse deeply political crises with substitute gratifications, the story becomes a version of what Jameson might call "the modernist project" (1981: 266). The theme of the story appears to be an anticolonialist allegory in which the adventurers are an absurd parody of the British in the third world; yet its apparent absurdity is subverted by imagery and language that idealize the imperial mission. And the distance of the frame, which appears at first to counter the inner, individual and subjective experience, finally supports it through its own neutralizing of irony with compassion.

The conflict between the realistic frame and the romantic story for which it provides a matrix, its two conflicted modes and genres, is partially generated by the historical contradiction of imperial culture: the myth of imperialism is disrupted by the very principle that created it—by colonial man who is neither god nor king, and by the colonized country (Kafiristan) that has already a power, a native presence, and a mother lodge which cannot tolerate the reality of the man beneath the myth.

The doubleness and splitting of the narrator mirror, the splitting of the colonial enterprise into agencies of protection and power, of subjugation and powerlessness. The narrator's office and life are invaded by the two adventurers who overpower him with their physical presence and demand his submission to their wishes; but his powerlessness is only temporary because he and his writing will survive into the permanence of recorded fiction. It mirrors too the splitting of Dravot from the ordinary man to the symbolic and divine God-King, a moment that is illuminated by Pierre Bourdieu's reading of political fetishism, "the process in terms of which individuals constitute themselves ... as a group but through this process lose control of the group in and through which they constitute themselves" (1984–5: 57). Dravot as political fetish consecrates himself with the mystery of leadership through strategies of language and action that ritualize his power. In Bourdieu's scheme, his splitting of the self is necessary to achieve "the oracle effect" through which the individual extinguishes himself in the service of the transcendent and symbolic self. The movement from man to king involves a conversion through which the ordinary person must die so that the symbolic moral person can be born (p. 63).

Whereas the outer story is told by a man about men, the inner story is a temporarily realized dream of heroism and kingship. The man who would be king, Dravot, focuses on the end product—kingship—as the basic unit of his economy around which all else must revolve. But he grows blind to those who grant him that kingship and upon whose labor his status depends. And it is that blindness to his people, to their expectations of him as king, that leads him to his fatal mistake—the marriage that exposes him as a man—a category which his kingship was designed to conceal. The impossible contradiction he is now faced with is quite simple: he cannot be both man and king and trust therefore die. Ironically, however, these polarities have been generated by his own desire and are as radically incompatible as those other binary oppositions that the convenient closure of the frame seeks to transcend—native and ruler, the individual and society, nature and culture, the unconscious and the conscious.

The frame narration creates an almost Brechtian estranging effect, at once alienating the reader from the subject matter and compelling her, in spite of the disturbing ambivalence of the narrator, to think about the political dimensions of the enclosed tale. The daring, swashbuckling, romantic adventure into Kafiristan is in part a projection of a narrator who cleaves to the security of margins, of offices, of bureaucracy, and of second-hand reporting of the forbidden adventures of others. But it is also what a Jameson might see as the nostalgic fantasy of an empire in crisis, creating for itself a myth of origins and trying to discover a cause for the still to be dreaded future—the fall of the

British Raj. The story of two crazy adventurers will become signs for the tragedy of colonialism: crucified by the men over whom they rule, their end will justify and glorify the means they use to attain it.[1] But it will also be a sign of the Kipling narrator's deepest fear which repeats itself with variations in poems and stories and dreams—the fear of literally and figuratively losing one's head; the story, then, is also an effort to master a recurring fear of self-loss.

NOTE

1. For other readings of "The Man Who Would Be King," see Manfred Draudt, who argues (unconvincingly) for a Laingian reading of Peachey's madness, in "Reality or Delusion? Narrative Technique and Meaning in Kipling's 'The Man Who Would Be King,'" *English Studies* 69 (1984): 316–26. See also Thomas Shippey and Michael Short who attempt a linguistic reading of multiple frames as ironic commentary on events and as a method of raising doubt about the reliability of both Carnehan and the "I" narrator in "Framing and Distancing in Kipling's 'The Man Who Would Be King,'" *The Journal of Narrative Technique*, 2 (1972): 58–87; and Jeffrey Meyers (*Fiction and the Colonial Experience.* Ipswich: The Boydell Press, 1973) and Benita Parry (*Delusions and Discoveries: Studies on India in the British Imagination 1880–1930.* Berkeley: University of California Press, 1972), who emphasize the moral failures of the adventurers as caricatures of colonialists but ignore the rhetorical complexities of Kipling's discourse. The finest reading of the story, to which all subsequent readings of Kipling's ironic use of the Bible are indebted, is Paul Fussell's "Irony, Freemasonry and Humane Ethics in Kipling's 'The Man Who Would Be King,'" *ELH* 25 (1958): 216–33.

> —Zohreh T. Sullivan, *Narratives of Empire: The Fictions of Rudyard Kipling*, (Cambridge: Cambridge University Press, 1993): pp. 99–102.

HELEN PIKE BAUER ON THE STORY'S AMBIGUOUS ATTITUDE TOWARD IMPERIALISM

[Helen Pike Bauer is Chair of the English Department at Iona College. Among other publications, she is the author of *Rudyard Kipling: A Study of the Short Fiction*. In this extract, she further elucidates how the story avoids easy interpretation.]

Kipling's stories of Anglo-India reveal a profound understanding of the instability of the English position. One of Kipling's most famous tales, "The Man Who Would Be King" (*PR*), embodies imperial pretensions in shifting lights. This rich story is virtually a farrago of imperial ideas, some presented sympathetically, some in parody, and some in tones too complex and unsteady to be labeled simply.[12] The exploits of Peachey Taliaferro Carnehan and Daniel Dravot, two ne'er-do-well, itinerant adventurers, are presented to us through an intermediary, an unnamed narrator; although a narrative frame is a favorite device of Kipling, it functions here in particularly complicated ways. The narrator, an Anglo-Indian newspaperman, is drawn into Peachey and Dan's story by agreeing to deliver a message from one to the other. He is later pressed to help them plan their adventure by supplying encyclopedias and maps of the area they wish to explore. Finally, he is the audience to whom the survivor, Peachey, tells his tale. Both a marginal accomplice and an objective listener, drawn in sympathy by the energy and daring of the men's vision, but repelled by its audacity and foregone failure, the narrator hears, witnesses, participates in, and comments on the story he tells us.

That story recounts Peachey and Dan's excursion into Kafiristan, unexplored territory in northern Afghanistan, of their desire to establish themselves as kings, to conquer and rule the natives, to accumulate wealth and power. And they accomplish all their aims. By arming and training small groups of natives who then form their defense against the rest of the population, by establishing their own authority and putting an end to petty tribal wars, by drawing on the Masonic traditions they and the natives know, by using their wits to impress the credulous primitive people, they become rulers in Kafiristan; Dan Dravot indeed becomes a king.

Peachey and Dan, while ambitious and daring, are themselves astonished at their success. They subjugate the natives through military might and political annexation, but they solidify their victory when they discover that their subjects know Masonic lore. The adventurers use their superior knowledge and the respect it brings them to win permanent obeisance. They have learned that true power is held not merely by guns but by using the culture of the powerless to support one's regime. "'Peachey,' says Dravot, 'we don't want to fight no more. The Craft's the trick, so help me!'" and Dravot's ambitions grow. "'I won't make a Nation,' says he. 'I'll make an Empire!'"

Peachey and Dan become simultaneously representatives and parodies of the Empire builders Kipling elsewhere idealizes. They employ the methods of the imperialist—military, political, cultural—but do so only for personal aggrandizement. Peachey and Dan represent an attempt at Empire without the moral values that, to Kipling, validate that attempt. They lack commitment to the native population, to standards of justice, to honor. And the story reveals the fate of imperial designs without a moral center: Peachey and Dan are attacked by their troops: Dan is killed, Peachey tortured and released to die.

But Kipling's story resists an easy condemnation of Peaches and Dan. They are, in many ways, sympathetic characters. Energetic, bold, imaginative, with a sense of humor and a delight in their own talent, they win the reader's interest and assent, even as they forfeit approval. And they are faithful to each other. Knowing he will be killed, Dan urges Peachey to flee, but Peachey responds, "Go to Hell, Dan! I'm with you here." Because they are not so much villains as rogues, they never fully embody the dark side of imperialism. Moreover, Kipling's complex narrative frame prevents our dismissing Peachey and Dan. The narrator's ambivalent response becomes ours, and, when Peachey returns to tell his tale, the vivid evidence of his intense suffering—his physical scars and mental fragility, his moving in and out of sane discourse—creates an affecting portrait. "The Man Who Would Be King" is one of Kipling's most analyzed stories; there is no doubt it contains a searching exploration of the dangers of imperial ambition, but it hedges that investigation by implicating the narrator and the reader. We sympathize with the adventurers while we see their exploitation of others. Again, as so often in his portraits of the Empire, Kipling creates a complex, distanced story whose ultimate attitude toward the events it depicts remains somewhat mysterious.

Peachey and Dan look on the natives of Kafiristan as simply

people to be subdued in order to promote their own authority. And if Kipling investigates the effects of imperialism on the imperialist, his attitude toward the native Indian population, as it operates in his fiction, is the second crucial aspect of his conception of imperialism that must be considered. There is no doubt that mixed with the good imperial England thought it was doing in India was a profound assumption that the Indians were a more primitive people, unwilling or unable to govern themselves, a teeming populace of races and castes in need of the rationality and efficiency that the West, particularly the Anglo-Saxon West, could provide. In essence, Kipling shared this view. At its highest it celebrated the good the English could do, often at great cost to themselves; at its worst, it supported and promoted a brutal racism.

NOTE

12. The story has accumulated a considerable body of criticism and provides a good example of the spectrum of approaches to Kipling's work. It is treated in virtually every full-length study as well as in numerous periodical essays. For a reading that focuses on the effect of the narrative frame, for example, see Tim Bascom, "Secret Imperialism: The Reader's Response to the Narrator in 'The Man Who Would Be King'," *English Literature in Transition, 1880–1920* 31 (1988): 162–73. Jeffrey Meyers, on the other hand, stresses the tale's straightforward exploration of imperialism; see "The Idea of Moral Authority in 'The Man Who Would Be King'," *Studies in English Literature* 8 (1968): 711–23.

—Helen Pike Bauer, *Rudyard Kipling: A Study of the Short Fiction*, (New York: Twayne, 1994): pp. 39–41.

"Without Benefit of Clergy"

Originally published in the June 1890 edition of *Macmillan's Magazine*, and among the stories collected the following year for *Life's Handicap*, "Without Benefit of Clergy" is regarded by most critics as the best of Kipling's tales of interracial love. The story displays a depth of feeling and emotional sincerity that Kipling seldom matched elsewhere in his work. At its center lies perhaps the most "Kiplingesque" of all his themes—man's futile effort to thwart and control the forces of chaos.

John Holden is the principal protagonist. A minor English civil servant living in India, who takes pleasure in neither his work nor the obligatory company of his fellow colonists, Holden's one joy is spending time with Ameera, a sixteen-year-old Muslim girl whom he had purchased several years before from her mother. Kipling never tells us whether Holden's original motive for buying the girl was practical, sexual, or to save her from an avaricious and uncaring mother, but it is clear from the outset that Ameera has risen above the status of slave, or even concubine. She is given a well-furnished house to share with her mother and it is there, behind its gated walls, that Holden takes refuge from the tedium and futility of his work and all the sickness, famine, and death that are so ever-present in Kipling's India.

The story begins with Ameera invoking one of many rituals that Kipling uses to represent the Eastern, or spiritual, method of coping with uncertainty and blind fate. This dependence on prayer and ritual is paralleled by the English/Western reliance on reason, bureaucratic protocol, and civic duty, as embodied by Holden and his Anglo associates. Neither, ultimately, proves effective. In assuring Holden that the child she is carrying is a boy, Ameera is also hoping to further endear herself and stave off the abandonment that both she and her mother consider inevitable. Holden does his best to convince Ameera that she has nothing to fear, and yet he is secretly so certain that sickness will take her while he is away on business that he fills out a telegram to that effect and gives it to Pir Khan, the watchman, to send when the time comes. Thus, in the opening section, Kipling establishes a precarious balance between anticipation and anxiety, love and doubt, which perfectly captures the bittersweet nature of any relationship, but particularly between people of different races living in a society that would condemn them.

The first section ends with the birth of Holden's son, an event surrounded by more ritual. Once again, Indian and English ways of dealing with change are contrasted, but now Holden is implicated in both. Having fathered a biracial child, he is now straddling both worlds. He steps on the dagger in the threshold and he sacrifices the goats and yet, "full of riotous exaltation," he also falls back on old habits by retreating to the club and shooting a game of pool. Nonetheless, the blood on his boots betrays a breach between the carefully segregated hemispheres of his life.

Part two of the story is delimited by the short lifespan of Holden and Ameera's son, Tota, a perfect embodiment of life's tenuousness. The absolute center of the story is the scene on the roof, where father, mother, and child count the stars and seize a timeless moment of utter contentment, beautifully expressed in Kipling's shimmering prose. The spell is broken when Ameera reveals that she has been praying to both Muhammad and "Beebee Miriam" (the Virgin Mary) to take her life, if death is demanded, instead of her lover or child. The significance here is twofold: firstly, Tota's and Ameera's deaths are being foreshadowed. Merely speaking Death's name in a Kipling story is tantamount to prophecy. Secondly, in her adoption of Christian as well as Muslim prayer practices, Ameera is revealing her own process of hybridization (though Mary is actually revered in the Muslim faith, Kipling underscores her essentially Western designation with Ameera's use of the words "thy Beebee Miriam" and her lingering belief that "it is not seemly for men to worship a woman"). Unfortunately, neither religion can protect them and baby Tota dies from "seasonal autumn fever," an inexorable-sounding malady if there ever was one. Holden reacts to Tota's death much the same way he did to his birth, by retreating to the English compound and numbing himself with protocol.

In part three, Holden and Ameera attempt to work through their grief and recover some measure of their former happiness, but Ameera is full of self-reproach and more convinced than ever that ritual and humility are the only way to appease God and avoid further tragedy. Kipling parallels her ineffectual superstitions by introducing the Member for Lower Tooting, a farcical bureaucrat who strides about in completely inappropriate attire, commits cultural faux pas, and then takes "his enlightened self out of India" when a passenger dining next to him on a ship is stricken with cholera. To further drive home the cold hard fact of Fate's unassailable power over the lives of his characters, Kipling personifies Nature as a sober and competent clerk who dutifully "audit[s] her accounts with a red pencil" and (when starvation doesn't enact the requisite debits) unleashes a plague of cholera upon the city. "Hindoo temples screamed and bellowed" and "the call to prayer from the minarets was almost unceasing" and still the "gods were inattentive in those days."

Holden begs Ameera to head for the hills like the white "*mem-log*" (women) but, in a final assertion of her cultural identity, she refuses to leave her "lord" behind. Hemmed in by sickness and death, they finally drop all ritual pretense, enjoy their time together, and call "each other openly by every pet name that could move the wrath of the gods." Here, in the same paragraph, Kipling encapsulates the entire story in a single sentence: "There are not many happinesses so complete as those that are snatched under the shadow of the sword." The sword does eventually fall, of course, and Ameera dies of cholera, but her last words aren't prayers or protestations but a testament to the supreme divinity of love: "I bear witness ... that there is no God but—thee, beloved."

Like many of Kipling's titles, "Without Benefit of Clergy" is an elaborate pun. Historically, the phrase refers to the 12th-century legal exemption that protected English clergyman (and later, anyone proving themselves literate) from criminal prosecution. In this sense, the title could refer to the fact that Holden is (perhaps unfairly) spared from the premature death that takes his Indian lover and child. More literal, however, is the phrase's ironic description of their union. Unconsecrated by any religious ceremony, Holden and Ameera nonetheless experience a degree of happiness, passion, and love not often attained in "holy wedlock." Those are the two meanings of the title most often mentioned, but there is a third that relates to the story's larger theme. Kipling seems to be saying that we are all "without benefit of clergy" in that, though they may bring temporary comfort and hope, no rituals, religions, or well-run bureaucracies can protect us from the fickle whims of Fate. Only love bequeaths any true happiness, and even that is fleeting. Holden and Ameera tried their best to establish an earthly haven, but in the end it was only temporal and "no man may say where [their] house stood."

"Without Benefit of the Clergy"

John Holden is the minor English civil servant who defies social convention, falling in love and having a child with a sixteen-year-old Indian girl who he has purchased from her mother. Whether the brief happiness he experiences is worth the final heartbreak is left open to debate.

Ameera is the young but headstrong Indian girl who bears Holden an ill-fated son. Ameera's reliance on prayer and ritual, her fatalist attitude towards her relationship with Holden, and her feelings toward the "white *mem-log*" (English women) provide glimpses into the minds of Indian women under colonial rule. Yet her dying words speak to a more universal truth.

Ameera's Mother is a cold and rapacious woman who sells her daughter to avoid penury, lives in comfort in the house of the man who has bought her, and cares for little more than how much of the furniture she can keep after her daughter's death.

Pir Khan is the kindly old watchman who guards the gates of the house shared by Holden and Ameera. His compassion and loyalty and his humble, non-materialistic reaction to the loss of his livelihood provides a foil to the selfishness of Ameera's Mother.

Ahmed Khan is the butler at Holden's private bungalow and another sympathetic servant.

The Member for Lower Tooting is a clueless English bureaucrat who tries to assert the "benefits of British rule" and then flees India at the first sign of danger.

"Without Benefit of Clergy"

J.M.S. TOMPKINS ON THE STORY'S CIRCULAR
STRUCTURE

[J.M.S. Tompkins was a noted literary critic, Professor of
English, and author of *The Popular Novel in English:
1770–1800*, as well as the seminal study *The Art of Rudyard
Kipling*. In this extract from the latter, Tompkins diagrams
the story's structure as a series of concentric circles.]

The reader who turns straight from 'Without Benefit of Clergy'
to 'The Gardener' can see very clearly what has been gained and
lost. Both are tales of love and secrecy, a secrecy that is imposed
by social conditions; and there the resemblance stops. 'Without
Benefit of Clergy' covers some three years, during which the
Mohammedan girl, whom John Holden has bought and now
loves as his wife, bears him a son in the little house over the city,
loses the child and finally dies of cholera. The narrative moves
smoothly from scene to scene, making unhurried use of dialogue
and joining the incidents with explicit narration and occasional
comment. The scene lies before us, as it were, in concentric
circles. At the centre is the native house; all the pictorial details,
the colours, the little homely sounds belong to this centre; here
we listen to the language of love and grief. Outside, continuously
indicated but never described, is John Holden's official life, the
Club, the Office, the 'unlovely' bungalow, open to any visitor, the
unsparing short phrases of order and criticism, edged with irony
by the unseen facts of the native house. It is in this circle that we
get the sarcasm—'cheap' sarcasm, since it is what any man's mind
and tongue will produce under the pressure of circumstances and
the infection of sympathy. Here, too, we get an unwished,
though not quite irrelevant, appearance of the obsessive Member
for Lower Tooting. Enclosing everything is the India of

swarming life and terrifying epidemics, generating the menace and finally the certainty of separation. The ties that penetrate all three circles meet in Ameera's room. Most of the scenes in the little house are night-pieces. This is natural, and it emphasizes the dichotomy of Holden's life; it also shows up the radiant beauty of Ameera as Juliet's is shown when she 'hangs upon the cheek of night like a rich jewel'. It is only at the end, when the hostility of nature has broken into the house, that we see its desolation in the daylight. The tragic forces in the tale are impersonal; no malice or even callousness is involved, though John Holden, in his anguish, calls himself a brute. The brief and beleaguered tenure of human happiness is made more apparent by the difference between the lovers, and the secrecy and irony that arise from it. They themselves are only sufficiently developed for the purposes of lyrical emotion, which requires figures and attitudes rather than characters. The tenderness of the hidden household reaches outside, and John Holden, in his first dealings with love and death, has brothers in Ahmed Khan, his butler, and his portly Indian landlord, who closes the tale. Holden's life is not concluded, but this episode is concluded, abolished, leaving nothing but the lacquer bed that Pir Khan, the old gate-keeper, warns him will be to him a knife turning in a green wound.

There are imperfections in this tale. Kipling's insatiable appetite for fact and strong excitement makes him divert our gaze too long towards the cholera-stricken multitudes, with a blurring of focus; and some readers may find the 'ordinary' quality of the sarcasm disturbing, as if Romeo, instead of 'Then I defy you, stars', had said 'Just what *would* happen'. But flawlessness is not what we can expect from the strongly creative writer in his copious youth, but that he shall convey his vision memorably. This Kipling does, and the flaws are no obstruction to our perception of beauty, death, and the hard necessities of daily work.

—J.M.S. Tompkins, *The Art of Rudyard Kipling* (London: Methuen, 1959): pp. 115–116.

[The late Elliot Gilbert was a longtime Professor of English at the University of California, Davis, and before that at Brooklyn College and Columbia. He is the author of the full-length study, *The Good Kipling*, and editor of *"O Beloved Kids": Rudyard Kipling's Letters to His Children* and *Kipling and the Critics*. The following excerpts his penetrating essay on the ontological conflict at the heart of the story.]

The failure of ritual, a fact which is central to the meaning of "Without Benefit of Clergy," is inevitable given ritual's function, to achieve order in a chaotic world. Different men, of course, conceive of this function in different ways. On the one hand, comparatively primitive people turn to ritual as a means of ordering the physical universe. They long to control the forces of life and in their elaborate ceremonies, they often seem to be presenting to the universe models of behavior in the forlorn hope that the universe will comply and shape itself a little closer to their desires. More sophisticated men, on the other hand, who have surer if less melodramatic methods of dealing with nature, nevertheless persist in their own adherence to ritual, not so much because they think it will help them to organize the universe as because they hope that it will help them to establish a little order in themselves. In either case, however, the passion for order is a key to the understanding of ritual.

In this connection, there is a revealing passage early in "Without Benefit of Clergy" in which Holden, thinking seriously for the first time of the child that is to come, finds that he cannot help but feel uneasy. "And there was going to be added to this kingdom a third person whose arrival Holden felt inclined to resent. It interfered with his perfect happiness. It disarranged the orderly peace of the house that was his own." If Holden's reaction is not all that a storybook father's should be, it at least has the virtue of being honest and, in addition, of being thoroughly in character. For Holden, we must not forget, is a young man who has come out to India to do something about the sprawling subcontinent, the huge, confusing country which, with its teeming masses of people and its violence and disease, is the ultimate metaphor for chaos, just as the British administrative passion is a striking metaphor for man's desire to impose order on confusion. Thus, in longing for order and peace in his own house, Holden is only longing for what all men desire and what they often find it necessary to invent rituals to achieve.

But order, seen in these terms, seems such a thoroughly respectable goal. If it is indeed order that is the object of ritual, can this same order also be the reason for ritual's failure? In "Without Benefit of Clergy," as in many other of his stories, Kipling seems to be suggesting that this is so. Not that he is sentimental about confusion and incompetence. That is the last thing in the world he can be accused of. Order obviously has its place, as the many successes of the British in India testify. There is nothing in the least edifying, for example, about famine, and so we read with a certain satisfaction that "on the heels of the spring-reapings came a cry for bread, and the Government, which had decreed that no man should die of want, sent wheat."

Such an example of control on the political level is certainly to be applauded, and Kipling, as much as any writer, has been quick to celebrate the man of action, the bridge-builder, the engineer, the administrator. But "Without Benefit of Clergy" is not a story about politics. To be sure, in the concentric worlds which surround the little house in the city, policy is everyone's concern. At the club, for instance, the talk is always "beating up round the ever-fresh subject of each man's work." But such talk remains always in the background; we hear very little of it. What we do hear constantly in this story is the long, sometimes interrupted but always renewed, conversation of Holden and Ameera as the two talk together in their room or on the roof of their house about the inexplicable way of the world and about the inordinate difficulty of coming to terms with it. And it is on this level, this personal level, that ritual fails most conspicuously in the story, because, as Kipling shows us, it is on this level that a passion for order is most fruitless and corrupting.

Why this should be so is not difficult to see. A passionate love of order inevitably implies a certain distaste for the truth about the world as it is actually constituted, implies a great longing to substitute for the disorganized reality of today, the perfectly structured artifice of tomorrow. How else explain the Englishman's willingness to die for the India of his plans and schemes and projects, and yet his refusal to accept the Indians, like Ameera, of the here and now? But the cluttered and untidy reality of the present so easily dismissed by orderly men—what is it, Kipling seems to be asking, but the only reality there is? Love, however much one may anticipate it for the future, can only be experienced in the present (the author tries to show), and life, however much one plans it better for tomorrow, can only be lived today. What's more, a law of compensation seems inevitably to apply to life, decreeing that any provision made for the future must be made at the expense of the present, so that no man may grow rich taking money from one pocket and putting it into another.

Ameera, for one, is quick to recognize the operation of this law. For much of the story she is bitter at the thought of how Englishwomen live longer and retain their youth and beauty longer than Indian women do. Always in her mind is the thought that she will soon be old and ugly and that Holden will leave her for one of the *mem-log*. Indeed, when we first meet her she is extremely self-conscious about her status, and her insistence upon defining herself in terms of the white lady seems to be one of her most important rituals. But when she learns that the white women accomplish their miracle by leaving their husbands for the six months of the hot weather and by turning their children over to nurses, her envy turns to contempt, her ritual longing for status vanishes the way all her other rituals vanish in the course of the story as she comes to understand and to accept reality.

The activities of the *mem-log* astound as much as they disgust her. Why should a woman want to live long and be beautiful, she wonders, except for the love of her husband and children? And if this is so, what madness possesses her to give up both husband and children in order to prolong that life and beauty? What end can she hope to achieve by postponing the experience of love from today until tomorrow, especially in a random and irrational universe in which the chance is always great that there will be no tomorrow? From a purely practical point of view, of course, Ameera's own refusal to withdraw to the Hills may seem foolishly willful. But in the sense that it represents her passionate commitment to an idea, to the idea that life—infinitely precious and, from all she has seen of it, infinitely tenuous—is meaningful only when it is being lived, that same refusal is shown to be courageous and honest. Thus Kipling is not writing a story about the destructiveness of intermarriage in a society which frowns on it and enforces secrecy. Ameera does not, as one critic has put it, eat herself up in the process of envying the white woman. Her decision to remain behind in the plains with Holden is based not on embarrassment or fear but on love.

"Without Benefit of Clergy" contains other characters who, like the *mem-log*, have abandoned the reality of human love to pursue an ephemeral and empty security. Ameera's old mother is one, her key to order and control being the acquisition of money and possessions. Having early been left penniless, she solved her problem by selling Ameera to Holden and would, we are told, have sold her "shrieking to the Prince of Darkness if the price had been sufficient." Her reaction to her daughter's death is especially in character. The girl has hardly breathed her last when the old woman is at Holden, tormenting him unmercifully about the few sticks of furniture she hopes to inherit. "In her anxiety to take stock of the house fittings," Kipling tells us, "she forgot to mourn."

The English administrators at their clubs also suffer from a mistrust of life which shows up in an exaggerated concern for order and propriety. Their reticence and their insularity are only ritualistic ways of postponing or avoiding human experience. Involved as they are in their work, they are too preoccupied with the horrors of tomorrow to react today, too busy constructing safe imitations of their old life to appreciate, as Holden does, the reality that is all around them. For as Holden would be the first to admit, the disruption of his orderly home is a small price to pay for his son. Such reality, he has learned, is always to be preferred to artifice, and reassuring Ameera one evening, for the thousandth time, that he will never abandon her for one of the *mem-log*, he says "'I have seen fire balloons by the hundred. I have seen the moon, and—then I saw no more fire balloons.'"

Ritual, then, implies the sacrifice of what we have for what we think we would prefer, and it is Kipling's purpose in "Without Benefit of Clergy" to expose the terrible fraud of such sacrifice, to show how, in attempting to comfort and reassure us, it involves us instead in the insane tautology of giving up the very life we are trying to achieve. "'Strike!'" says Pir Khan to Holden, as the Englishman is about to sacrifice the two goats. "'Never life came into the world but life was paid for it.'" To which Holden replies with the words of the prayer, offering "'life for life, blood for blood, head for head, bone for bone, hair for hair, skin for skin.'"

But nothing will ever be gained, Kipling assures us, from bargains like this. It is not man's business to haggle with the universe (using his most precious commodity—life—as the medium of exchange) no matter what name he gives that haggling, no matter what ritualistic form it may take. It is man's business, rather, to live as richly as he can, postponing nothing, flinching at nothing, recognizing as inevitable that the more he has the more he will lose, that the greater his joy the greater will be his sorrow; yet sacrificing nothing out of cowardice or in the vain hope that he can find a happiness he will not have to pay for. This is the theme of "Without Benefit of Clergy."

In order to express so far-reaching a theme within the framework of a piece of fiction, Kipling has dramatically arrayed two powerful forces against one another. On one side there is a world full of fear and of rituals to drive out fear; there is India, burdened with death and with terror of the unknown, turning to religion and magic in a desperate attempt to find meaning and order in the universe; there are the English in their compound with their conventions and their forms, anxious to serve but too quick, in the name of self-sacrifice, to postpone living to a more auspicious time. On the other side there is the small house in the midst of the city; there is the poignancy of the feeling Holden and Ameera have for one another; there is the child who incarnates their love; there is Holden with his refreshing desire to move beyond the narrow, official experiences of his peers; and most of all, there is Ameera.

—Elliot Gilbert, "'Without Benefit of Clery': A Farewell to Ritual." *Kipling and the Critics* (New York: New York University Press, 1965): pp 171–176.

JEFFREY MEYERS ON THE "WHITE MAN'S CODE"

[Jeffrey Meyers has taught English at several universities, including UCLA and the University of Colorado. He is the author of numerous books, including biographies of Orwell, Hemingway, Conrad, and Poe, as well as *Privileged Moments: Encounters with Writers* and *The Biographer's Art*. In this excerpt, Meyers disagrees with Gilbert and interprets the story as an allegory of what happens to those who break the "White Man's Code."]

The tender love of Ameera and Holden, which in the early part of "Without Benefit of Clergy" (*Life's Handicap*, 1891) appears to be so beautiful and perfect, and which reaches its apotheosis in the wonderfully lyrical nocturne as they sit by the low white parapet of the roof overlooking the city and its lights, is unable to transcend their racial differences and successfully fuse both cultures. Gilbert surely misinterprets the story when he states, "in the last analysis the title represents Kipling's approval of the couple, of their life together".[1] On the contrary, their union is destroyed by cultural conflicts, both internal and external, which find expression in the doubts, anxieties and fears of the lovers, who suffer the visitation of fever, cholera and finally the physical destruction and total annihilation of their house as a fatal retribution for breaking every rule and law of the while man's axle. Their love becomes all the more poignant when it is viewed as a brief and pathetic interlude before the inevitable punishment.

Though Ameera and Holden have been happily "married", albeit without benefit of clergy, ceremony or church, for two years when the story opens, Ameera is afraid of losing Holden. "How could I be sure of thy love," she asks Holden in the first lines. "when I knew that I had been bought with silver?" She is joyous about the birth of her son, not only for the usual reasons, but also because she (and her mother) feel her son will bind her elusive and shadowy husband to her.[2] One of the many ironies of the story is that the birth and sudden death of their son, the living embodiment of their union whose body unites the blood of the two races, marks the beginning of their doom.

Ameera also fears "the *mem-log*—the white women of thy own blood" who enjoy "benefit of clergy" in the sacramental as well as in the penal sense. It seems to Ameera that these privileged beings unjustly postpone the punishment of death and live for three times the length of her life. The white women escape death because they have the "benefit" of spending the unhealthy hot season in the hills, which Ameera refuses to have, for her love for Holden seems greater and stronger than that of any white woman in Kipling's stories. "How shall I depart," Ameera asks, "when I know that if evil befall thee by the breadth of so much as my littlest finger-nail is that not small?—I should be aware of it though I were in paradise?"

When Ameera tells Holden he has made her very English, she is speaking more truth than she realizes. This does not mean she has become anglicized like the bold white *mem-log*, but that she has completely accepted the English attitude toward miscegenation. She succumbs to the idea of white superiority (this is why she is so fearful and repeatedly tells Holden she is his servant and his slave, and would not have it otherwise. Her highest aspiration for her son is that he be not a pundit, but a trooper of the Queen since half-castes are barred from the officer class. What is for Holden merely a nursery-rhyme whim ("And if it be a boy he shall fight for his king"), is for Ameera a very real hope. When she is on her deathbed, as the first drops of rain bring shouts of joy in the parched city, Holden is transformed in her mind from absolute master into a divine god whom she alone worships and who replaces even Allah Himself. Her last words are a blasphemous variation of the traditional Islamic affirmation of faith, which she had whispered into her son's ear just after he was born: "I bear witness that there is no God but God" (*La Ilaha Illallah*). She now distorts this into "I bear witness ... that there is no God but—*thee*, beloved."

Unlike the English who are married in church and hope to be reunited after death, Ameera believes their religions will keep them apart after life as they did in life, and that they will be taken to strange and separate paradises. Perhaps this is why her grief overwhelms her love when her son dies, and she screams her regrets at Holden: "The white men have hearts of stone and souls of iron. Oh, that I had married a man of mine own people though he beat me—and had never eaten the bread of an alien."

Ameera's anxieties and fears are also shared by Holden who constantly anticipates Ameera's death, and has a foreboding of the inevitable doom that threatens his uneasy love. After his son is born he is filled with a dread of loss, and when the cholera comes he is absolutely certain Ameera will die. This dread and absolute certainty stem from his need to expiate the guilt he has incurred by breaking the Sahib's code and living with a native woman.

Holden seems to have acquired from Ameera a great deal of Moslem fatalism. This is inevitable when there is extremely high infant mortality and continuous epidemics, when the dead cart bears the corpses through the city gate each morning, when they are separated for twelve hours each day and she might die in three, and when the rains instantly turn dust into torrents of mud and scour open the shallow graves. With resolute acceptance of her fate, Ameera exclaims of her son's death, "it was written". And Holden's butler Ahmed Khan, who like all Indians has known much suffering, intuits Holden's grief and says: "the shadows come and go, sahib; the shadows come and go." Holden learns only too well to touch happiness with caution and to snatch joy under the shadow of the sword that takes life suddenly and without warning.

Just as Ameera has acquired certain English ways of thinking, so Holden has learned Moslem customs. When the watchman Pir Khan suggests a birth sacrifice to guard the newborn child from an evil fate, Holden decapitates the goals and mutters the Mohammedan prayer while raw blood spurts over his riding hoots. Like the dagger laid on the threshold of the baby's room to avert ill luck, which Holden breaks with his heel, the birth sacrifice is unable to prevent the child's death. These Moslem customs are ultimately meaningless and cannot unify Holden's "double life". The discordance of his two lives is symbolized when the men in the Club are upset by the blood on his boots.

These bloody hoots suggest the conflict between life with Ameera and the work, orders and duty which take Holden from her. There is a recurrent heaven–hell contrast between his dark empty bungalow and the Club where Holden must repress his emotions and hide all trace of his happiness; and his sleeping baby, the gentle bullocks, the croaking water pipe, the spinning, the music and the moonlight of the peaceful courtyard where he expresses his tenderness, joy and love. But when the child and Ameera die, these worlds are reverted. The peaceful courtyard becomes a hell of self-questioning reproach and work a welcome distraction from grief and despair. Kipling's men court disaster and tragedy when they commit themselves to love instead of work. (...)

Holden attempts to transcend the white man's code, but is unable to replace it with an alternative moral system of his own. There is an acknowledgment of shame and guilt in the way he accedes to the imperious necessity for hiding all trace of his powerful love for Ameera. The marriage is doomed to destruction, not by fatal fever and cholera, but rather by Kipling's sanction of the "colour prejudice" and "superiority complex of his age." The final irony is that Ameera's greatest fear may well come to pass as she had predicted: "When I die, or the child dies, what is thy fate? Living, thou wilt return to the bold white *mem-log*, for kind calls to kind."

NOTES

1. Elliot Gilbert, "'Without Benefit of Clergy': A Farewell to Ritual," *Kipling and the Critics*, ed. Elliot Gilbert (New York: Gotham, 1965), p. 181. Gilbert's interpretation follows that of Walter Hart who writes in *Kipling the Story-Writer* (Berkeley, 1918), p. 79, of Kipling's "desire to show the superiority of this irregular union over many regular marriages." Though this story has been frequently anthologized and highly praised—Somerset Maugham calls it "the best story Kipling ever wrote (*Maugham's Choice of Kipling's Best*, New York, 1953, p. xx)—only Hart and Gilbert have written extended evaluations of the tale. The following critics have devoted a short paragraph to this stork: Edmund

Wilson, "The Kipling That Nobody Read," *The Wound and The Bow* (New York: Galaxy, 1965), p. 96; Randall Jarrell, ed., *In the Vernacular: The English in India* (New York: Anchor, 1963), pp. xvi–xvii; J. M. Stewart, "Kipling," *Eight Modern Writers* (Oxford, 1963), p. 243; Bhaskara Rao, *Rudyard Kipling's India* (Norman, Okla., 1967), p. 101; and Bonamy Dobrée, *Rudyard Kipling: Realist and Fabulist* (New York, 1967), p. 63.

2. Though Ameera is very perceptive and realistic about the "marriage," both Hart (pp. 70–71) and J. M. S. Tompkins, *The Art of Rudyard Kipling* (London. 1959), p. 101, mistakenly emphasize her ignorance and lack of awareness.

—Jeffrey Meyers, "Thoughts on 'Without Benefit of Clergy'." *The Kipling Journal* 36, no.172 (1969): 8–11.

JAMES HARRISON ON WHAT AMEERA LEARNS

[James Harrison is Professor Emeritus of English at the University of Guelph, Ontario and the author of numerous articles on Victorian literature. In this extract from his full-length study, *Rudyard Kipling*, Harrison sheds some light on what Ameera learns at tale's end.]

A story which does have a claim to be his most remarkable piece of short fiction about Indians is the deeply moving and often praised "Without Benefit of Clergy," which tells of the marriage, however unblessed by clergy, of an Indian girl and an Anglo-Indian administrator. Written after Kipling's return to England, it is perhaps too bold to have first appeared in the *Pioneer*. Yet he had published several stories in India which treated of sexual relations between the races, the most striking being "Beyond the Pale." This opens with a platitude from the narrator which, along with the title, is clearly intended to elicit nods of sage approval: "A man should, whatever happens, keep to his own caste, race and breed" (1:189). Yet no reader, however much in agreement with such sentiments, can recall those words in the same frame of mind, once having read the story. Not when the horrifying fate of the fifteen-year-old Hindu widow, her relatives having discovered that she is being visited secretly by an Englishman, is contrasted with the casual if quite genuine pleasure the visitor takes in this unspoiled child of nature. The truth of the axiom has been more than amply demonstrated (and, with an added irony, demonstrated as a result of *Indian* intolerance). Yet it can no longer be subscribed to with the same complacency.

But to return to "Without Benefit of Clergy,"[8] the story tells of an Englishman's impulsively buying a young Indian girl from her greedy mother, of their growing love for one another, of how the birth of a son still further enriches their love as his death still further deepens it, and of the eventual death of the girl. It has been read as a cautionary tale exemplifying the same sad truth that a man should keep to his own caste, race, and breed;[9] if it had not been cholera it would have been slower but no less fatal social pressures which put an end to their love. But the love described is of the kind which takes its whole quality from the very fact of its being enjoyed for each moment's sake, irrespective of what the future brings. It is in fact intensified not only by the strangeness, the newness of each of the lovers for the other, and by the need to keep their life together a precarious secret, but also by the recurring threats to its permanence. Whether ended by cholera or social pressures or sheer old age, it will still have been worth the having, and whatever is lost as a result of it will have been well lost.

What neither of the lovers loses is his or her essential Englishness or Indianness, each rather adding something to it. John Holden still puts in an appearance at the club after returning from a temporary posting elsewhere, even though longing to see his wife and the child which has probably been born to him in the interim. Likewise, after a reunion almost too fraught with joy to be borne, he returns to the club to pull himself together, the blood of the goats he was required to sacrifice still on his boots. His own tribal rituals are still necessary. But they, and the reprimand he receives for not having had his mind on his work during his temporary posting, are viewed with a sense of proportion rare in Kipling, for whom rituals and the work ethic too often seem paramount. Similarly, Ameera continues to perform all the appropriate rituals for averting harm to the child's and their happiness. After the child's death, moreover, both parents are more secretive than ever about their love, as if to propitiate or avoid attracting the attention of whatever might begrudge them their joy in one another. When Holden offers to send her to the hills in the hot weather, however, she scorns this white woman's precaution against misfortune, if it means leaving her man behind. Life itself is so provisional a commodity in India that today's happiness is too precious to be traded for some hypothetically more lasting or worthwhile happiness tomorrow. So, when cholera strikes the city, they abandon the superstitious concealment of their love, "calling each other by every pet name that could move the wrath of the gods." At last Ameera has recognized that, aside from that which there is no defense against, their happiness is threatened by and needs protection from no one but themselves. So much so that her dying words are, "I bear witness—I bear witness—that there is no god but—thee, beloved" (4:134).

NOTES

8. My reading of the story is strongly indebted to Elliot Gilbert's, pp. 21–41.

9. Noel Annan, "Kipling's Place in the History of Ideas," in Rutherford, pp. 110–11, and Dobrée, p. 63.

—James Harrison, *Rudyard Kipling* (Boston: Twayne, 1982): pp. 45–47.

HELEN PIKE BAUER ON KIPLING'S IMAGES OF ENCLOSURE

[In the following excerpt from her book on Kipling, Bauer surveys the story's literal and thematic enclosures.]

"Without Benefit of Clergy," like "Beyond the Pale," works with barriers and boundaries and enclosed spaces, but to very different effect. Again we pass from the vague, relatively undefined outside world of the Anglo-Indian civil servant into the private world of the Indian, but Kipling's descriptions are much more specific here. We move into the red-walled city, through the courtyard, past a wooden gate to the house of Ameera, the sixteen-year-old girl John Holden bought two years before the story begins. But Ameera's room is no prison, and she is no mere courtesan; the narrator insists the room is a palace and that Holden and Ameera are king and queen.

These two create their own world, and it is richly described. We see the bedroom's furnishings, its red-lacquered couch, floor cloths, and cushions. We are given an elaborate portrait of Ameera wearing her best clothes, her diamond nose stud, the flawed emeralds and rubies in her forehead ornament, her gold necklace and silver anklets, her jade-green muslin gown. Though she is poor, we see Ameera through her own and Holden's eyes, shining in color and grace, and deeply happy. And at night, she and Holden and their infant son, Tota, climb to the roof of the house to count the stars. The celestial system itself becomes part of the kingdom Ameera and Holden create.

But Holden leads a double life. He spends his nights with Ameera in the house he rents for her and his days at work. Yet his public existence has little meaning for Holden; he enjoys the club life, to be sure, but his work is unsatisfying, a distraction, something he performs poorly and cares little for. He rushes home at the end of each day to Ameera, and the grayness of his public days is contrasted with the intense color of his private nights.

But Holden and Ameera's life together is doomed. Although she fears Holden must eventually return to the English world, take an English wife, and leave his Indian idyll behind, Ameera does not live to see her fears realized. First Tota becomes ill and dies of "the seasonal autumn fever." Kipling's term, so matter of fact, makes Tota's death seem one of many, almost to be expected. Though Ameera and Holden do their best to comfort each other, the rigors of the Indian climate attack again. Cholera becomes epidemic. Because their life is secret and unsanctioned by the government, Holden cannot send Ameera to the hill station for protection. His efforts to persuade her to go on her own to the mountains are unsuccessful. She prides herself on a fidelity that surpasses that of the self-absorbed English women. She stays in the city, contracts the disease, and dies in Holden's arms.

From the beginning of the story, Ameera and Holden have tried to appeal to and placate the gods. She especially prays for a son, prays for a healthy child, prays that her life be taken before

Holden's or the child's. But the gods do not protect Ameera; nor does nature, which brings drought and disease; nor does society, which despises such as her. The forces that surround the life she creates with Holden pierce the boundaries, enter the house, and destroy what is valuable within. In her dying words, Ameera forswears those things in which she formerly placed her trust, amulets and charms, rituals and prayer. "'I bear witness—I bear witness'—the lips were forming the words on his ear—'that there is no God but—thee, beloved!'" Only the personal life they have created is of value to Ameera. No force outside their love can protect or comfort.

As Ameera dies, the long-awaited rains arrive with torrents of water and driving winds. Three days later, Holden, who is about to be transferred, returns to Ameera's house. It has been beaten down by the deluge, the pillars destroyed, the gate torn from its hinge, "as if the house had been untenanted for thirty years instead of three days." For it was Ameera who animated the house; she, like Holden, possessed the spark of divinity that gives life. Without her, the house collapses. Holden's landlord declares, in sympathy, that he will tear down any part that remains standing, "so that no man may say where this house stood." All evidence of the love Ameera and Holden bore each other will he obliterated.

The store uncompromisingly elevates the dignity and value of the private love Ameera and Holden share over any external set of conventions. Here is a world where, seemingly, the social structures that separate the races are surmountable. But the victory, though profound, is evanescent. For the Indian girl and Anglo-Indian man live in a world where outside forces ultimately reign. Kipling's story does not patronize or infantilize the Indian; rather, Ameera teaches Holden the sanctity of the inner life, the hollowness of the outer. But both characters are fated to suffer. For the private world cannot long endure without the support of the public. The secrecy of Holden's family life means he is continually separated from Ameera; he is, in his superior's eyes, a bachelor, easily transferred to new posts when a short-term substitute is needed. And the structures that would have helped Ameera and Tota, removal to a better climate, medical care, are unavailable to this clandestine family. If Ameera and Holden's love seems sweeter because it is private, its narrow circumscription makes it vulnerable and intensifies its pain. At the story's end, in his suffering, Holden must yet go back to work alone, unable to speak of the disaster his life has become.

Kipling's images of space and enclosure define a protected place where private safety and pleasure can exist apart from a threatening frontier. Most often, in the Indian stories, the enclosed space is that of the Raj. But here he reverses the pattern; it is the public world that threatens this private garden where psychic identity and joy can exist. The legally sanctioned world is barren; the illegitimate is sacred. And Kipling's title becomes ironic; Ameera and Holden reject the favors of convention. They suffer the mortal consequences, but their happiness surpasses any other even hinted at in the public world.

A story such as "Without Benefit of Clergy" undermines any attempt to interpret Kipling's view of the Empire as mere racist exploitation. There is no doubt he has many racist stories, that he often portrays Indians as children, incapable of making mature judgments about their lives, as intellectually inferior, morally, primitive, emotionally unstable. There is no doubt, too, that his major sympathies were with the English who traveled to India, often for mixed motives, but who were capable of great sacrifice and great good. But he also wrote of the hidden lives of Indians, of deep and lasting affection among lovers and families, of the hardships endured by those who live the lives of a subjugated people. Moreover, these stories, among those with Indian settings, contain virtually Kipling's only treatment of a rich and satisfying sexuality. The sexual drive of Kipling's Anglo-Indian characters seems feeble, narrow, and manipulative compared with that of his Indians. There is no Anglo-Indian equivalent to Ameera, whose inner sensuousness, complemented by her physical beauty, is fully integrated with her affections and becomes the mainstay of her life.

Some of Kipling's stories are hard to read today. They celebrate a point of view we find forbidding. But he is an artist with a rich sympathy for India and for those westerners who went out there to work. Ultimately, his view of the Empire, based on respect for practical labor, recognition of the value of community, belief in political order and social stability, is positive. But his profound understanding, evidenced in many stories, of the pain inflicted by imperialism, humanizes his beliefs. The existence of stories that treat that pain with tenderness must stand as a testimony to the complexity of Kipling's writings about the Empire.

—Helen Pike Bauer, *Rudyard Kipling: A Study of the Fiction* (New York: Twayne, 1994): pp. 47–50.

"Lispeth"

The first story in Kipling's first collection, written when he was in his early twenties, "Lispeth" is an oft-overlooked piece that contains early examples of several themes and techniques that inform many of his later works. The titular heroine is a "hill-girl" from the Kotgarh region of Northern India (near the Tibetan border), whose parents die of cholera, leaving her in the care of a missionary chaplain and his wife. Although Lispeth grows into a statuesquely beautiful, partly Westernized young woman, learning to read and dress as a European she retains the free-spirited and headstrong nature of her people. She refuses the suggestion of the chaplain's wife to move to a nearby town, "take service" as a nurse, and become more "genteel." Instead she develops a habit of taking arduous, daylong hikes by herself around the Himalayan countryside. During one such excursion, she happens upon a wandering English naturalist who has fallen from a cliff and badly cut his head. Lispeth rescues the man, single-handedly delivers him to the Chaplain and his wife, and matter-of-factly proclaims that she has found herself a husband. Horrified by the unladylike indiscretion of falling in love at first site, the Chaplain and his wife lecture Lispeth in the hopes of changing her mind. But she remains steadfast. Flattered by her attentions, the Englishman takes his time recuperating and does nothing to divest Lispeth of her romantic notions. As Kipling so succinctly puts it, "It meant nothing at all to him, and everything in the world to Lispeth."

Inevitably, the naturalist grows strong enough to return home, at which time the Chaplain's wife, "being a good Christian and disliking anything in the shape of fuss and scandal" advises him to placate Lispeth with a lie about plans to return and marry her. Several months later, when Lispeth's worry and frustration has reached a fever pitch, the chaplain's wife finally admits their collective deceit. Furious, Lispeth leaves the mission forever, returns to her people, marries an abusive woodcutter, and dies a bitter old woman.

In and of itself, this simple story barely warrants the ink required to summarize it. The "characters" are rather one-dimensional, the tone is didactic, and ultimately, Kipling's other stories of interracial love (see "Without Benefit of Clergy") are far more compelling. However, when judged in light of his entire body of work, certain aspects of "Lispeth" do provide important insights into Kipling's method, his attitudes toward missionaries and native peoples, and his literary development. The first is how Kipling's use of irony, further discussed in the critical extract by Martin Seymour-Smith, reveals a nascent interest in simultaneously entertaining his readers with a good story and engaging them in an intertextual debate. While the denser of his contemporary English readers might have overlooked the irony and simply interpreted the story as either an affirmation of their beliefs on miscegenation and the "White Man's Burden" or a quaint tragedy about true love lost, perceptive readers were forced to ask themselves just what good the missionaries brought to this girl's life and whether the same holds true for the imperialist enterprise as a whole. As Daniel Karlin has pointed out in his notes on the story (*Rudyard Kipling*, Oxford, 1999), Kipling lets the deserting Englishman off rather easy, reserving "his real hostility" for the missionaries. In support, Karlin quotes from a response Kipling gave to a secretary of the Board of Foreign Missionaries who had written him asking for a letter of support:

> "To tell the truth, no letter that I could write would in any way assist your cause ... It is my fortune to have been born and to a large extent brought up among those whom white men call 'heathen' and while I recognize the paramount duty of every white man to follow the teachings of his creed and conscience as 'a debtor to the whole law [Gal. 5:3],' it seems to me cruel that white men, whose governments are armed with the most murderous weapons known to science, should amaze and confound their fellow creatures with a doctrine of salvation imperfectly understood by themselves and a code of ethics foreign to the climate and instincts of

those races whose most cherished customs they outrage and whose gods they insult." (*The Letters of Rudyard Kipling*, vol. ii, 205–6)

Though in marked contrast to some of his later pronouncements, this quote reveals a man who is a far cry from the arch imperialist portrayed by Kipling's most ardent critics. So a second, related insight afforded by a reading of the story is how the characters of Lispeth and the missionaries reveal Kipling's conflicted sympathy for the colonized peoples of India.

The aspect many critics find most noteworthy about "Lispeth," however, is that thirteen years later Kipling reincarnated her as the Woman of Shamlegh in Chapter 14 of *Kim*. Instead of the tragic fate to which she was originally consigned, Kipling reintroduces her as a noble and fully liberated village leader who unashamedly tries to seduce Kim. It is almost as if Kipling felt compelled, out of guilt, to rewrite a new life for one of his earliest characters, but it also hints at larger issues concerning the rights of women and Indian natives. For more on the significance of Lispeth's return, see the critical extract by John A. McClure.

"Lispeth"

Lispeth is the beautiful hill-girl of the Himalayas who is raised, baptized, and partially Anglicized by a Christian missionary and his wife. Lispeth later appears as the "Woman of Shamlegh" in Kipling's novel *Kim*.

The Chaplain and his Wife are the narrow-minded missionaries who, shocked by the passion of Lispeth's love for the Englishman, advise him to lie to her about plans to return.

The Englishman is the traveling naturalist who, after he is rescued and recovered from his injuries, deceives Lispeth with false promises to return and marry her. He is also a good example of the kind of tourist that Kipling held in low regard.

"Lispeth"

ANGUS WILSON ON KIPLING'S HIMALAYAN FASCINATION

[Angus Wilson was a renowned author and educator who taught at several universities in England and the United States; published seven novels, three collections of short stories, and numerous works of non-fiction; and was made a Commander of the Order of the British Empire in 1968. In this excerpt from his biography of Kipling, Wilson traces the origins of the author's interest in Himalayan peoples.]

It is notable that, in [Kipling's] work and in his life, the peoples of the foothills of the Himalayas seem to share something of the great mountains' grace. In 1885, he made a recuperative journey there as far as 9,000 feet and was enchanted by the hill people and the beauty of their women. Here, one feels, are people who need nothing save protection from the white world. And, indeed, it is here that two stories are laid showing how absurd and empty, even harmful are the dreams of Christians who would seek to impose their beliefs upon the natives. In Kipling's eyes, this was never other than foolish throughout India, but here in these idyllic hill villages it is seen as actively cruel. "Lisbeth", the heroine of the story that stands first in *Plain Tales from the Hills*, becomes half servant, half companion to the chaplain's wife in Kotgargh. She meets and saves a young English traveller who has fallen by the wayside with fever. And she believes his loving professions of thanks. He will come back to her, and the chaplain and his wife, for the sake of peace, repeat the promise. "'How can what he and you said be untrue?' 'We said it as an excuse to keep you quiet, child,' said the chaplain's wife. 'Then you have lied to me? You and he?'" She goes, of course, back to her people. We are told that when she was an old, "bleached wrinkled creature, exactly like a wisp of charred rag, if she was sufficiently drunk, sometimes she could be induced to tell the story of her first love-affair".

Fourteen years later, in *Kim*, Kipling returned to Lisbeth, disturbed perhaps by the crude violence with which in his youth he had expressed his disgust at her treatment. In *Kim* we see her not as old and drunken but as the handsome ruler of her village people. But even then she can hope for no love from the white world. Kim cannot return her embrace, for he is still serving his discipleship to the Lama and his apprenticeship to the Game. Just as disastrous is the result of the mission of Justus Krenk, Pastor of the Tübingen Mission to the people of the Berbula Hills in "The Judgement of Dungara". This was written in 1888 before the Germans had acquired the satanic quality that they increasingly had for Kipling from 1890. They were seen as well-intentioned, plodding people. But their Mission in Berbula is a disaster as great as Dan and Peachey's kingdom. "The chapel and school have long since fallen back into the jungle," the story ends. But there is a difference, for "The Man Who Would Be King" ends in horror, while the Krenks are driven out by a rather schoolboyish joke (a tribal Stalkyism). It marks the difference of the hills of the Himalayas from the hills of the frontier—and of their inhabitants. It marks the two views of primitivism which alternate in Kipling's mind—half-devils who crucify and half-children who defeat by gigantic practical jokes. In various degrees, this mixture lies in most of the native Indian world which was the most powerful fictional love affair of his life.

—Angus Wilson, *The Strange Ride of Rudyard Kipling* (New York: Viking, 1978): pp. 91–92.

JOHN A. MCCLURE ON LISPETH'S REAPPEARANCE IN *KIM*

[John A. McClure is Professor of English at Rutgers University, specializing in colonial cultural studies. In the following two extracts, taken from his study of the works of Kipling and Conrad, McClure locates the story's place in Kipling's body of work.]

Kipling's early work suggests that his initial impulse was indeed toward exposure, exploration, and identification, but that this impulse was soon stifled. Throughout his writing career Kipling creates Indian characters and describes their motivations, but only in his earlier stories, those of the eighties, does he create sympathetic Indian characters who do not conform to orthodox imperial assumptions. The good Indians of the later stories either respect the British or criticize anti-imperialist elements in English society; the rest are fools or villains.

Yet one of Kipling's earliest published stories is a sympathetic portrayal of an Indian woman who rebels against her British superiors. "Lispeth" (1886) is about an Indian girl who becomes the protégée of Christian missionaries. Her own people ostracize her for adopting Western habits and values, but she endures this treatment gladly and grows every day in wisdom and knowledge. Then, having rescued an English traveler, she falls in love with him. She determines to marry the man, and neither he nor the missionaries have the decency to disillusion her. Only months after he has left does the chaplain's wife reveal the truth: "That the Englishman had only promised his love to keep her quiet— that he had never meant anything, and that it was wrong and improper of Lispeth to think of marriage with an Englishman, who was of superior clay."[22] Her illusions of British good faith and fraternity shattered, Lispeth rebels: "'I am going back to my own people,' said she. 'You have killed Lispeth. There is only left old Jadéh's daughter ... You are all liars, you English.'"[23]

Within the bounds of the story, there is nothing to contradict the justice of Lispeth's condemnation of the British, or to challenge her right to make it. Kipling insists on the truth of her original commitment to Western ideals, celebrates her love for the Englishman, sympathizes with her trust, and respects her reaction into traditionalism. Imperialism's promise to educate the colonized for equality is revealed as a hollow sham. Yet Kipling may not have intended so broad a criticism of imperial practice as I suggest. Significantly, the Englishmen on whom Lispeth bases her generalized condemnation belong to groups disliked by many imperialists and frequently criticized by Kipling: missionaries and tourists. Moreover, in later years Kipling attacks reformers for encouraging expectations of equality among the Indians. He argues that such promises are unrealistic and should not be made. But if this is his theme in "Lispeth," it is almost completely obscured by his admiration for the girl and his clear insistence on her superiority to her English guardians. Thus early in his writing career Kipling describes the imperial situation as seen by a betrayed and righteously indignant victim of the British. (...)

The last chapters of *Kim* are filled with gestures of inclusion that affirm Kim's status as a privileged member of the Indian family. Perhaps the most dramatic of these is Kim's symbolic union with the Woman of Shamlegh. After the struggle with the Russian spies, Kim and the lama retire to the mountain village of Shamlegh. The head of this village is an impressive Indian woman whose fondness for Kim leads her first to try to seduce him and then, when she realizes that he is bound to save the ailing lama, to give him valuable assistance.

This episode does not reveal its full significance unless the reader recognizes the Woman of Shamlegh as Lispeth, the heroine of the early Kipling story of the same name. The Woman's history, which she relates to Kim, recapitulates the plot of the earlier story: "'Once, long ago, if thou canst believe, a Sahib looked on me with favour. Once, long ago, I wore European clothes at the Mission-house Yonder.' She pointed towards Kotgarh. 'Once, long ago, I was *Ker-lis-ti-an* and spoke English—as the Sahibs speak it. Yes. My Sahib said he would return and wed me—yes, wed me. He went away—I had nursed him when he was sick—but he never returned'" (p. 431). Here is "Lispeth of the Kotgarh Mission," the heroine of the Kipling story most critical of imperial rule, reappearing after fourteen years.

Kipling reintroduces her at this time, I believe, in order to impress on us the superiority of country-bred rulers. Lispeth's pain, Kipling suggests in the earlier story, stems from the ignorance and aloofness of the English. Her lover does not recognize her as a fellow human being, nor does he accept the obligations such a recognition would entail. Instead, he takes her love and deludes her as to his own feelings, while all the time planning his return to England and to his English fiancée. His careless betrayal of a marriage pledge suggests the larger betrayal of the Indian people by their English rulers.

Kipling has Kim meet Lispeth to show that such betrayals are not inevitable. Kim's situation resembles that of the earlier European: he is aided and wooed by Lispeth in much the same way. But whereas the earlier figure, repaying kindness with deception, makes pledges he does not plan to keep, Kim deals with the Woman of Shamlegh frankly, fairly, and generously. She wants him as a lover, and he apparently refuses her, but he does reveal his true identity in an embrace and a kiss, for which she blesses him. And when she gives him money, he is careful to see it restored to her.

The full significance of their relationship emerges in the echoes set off by her last question, "you will come back again?" (p. 435). These words, recalling the faithlessness of her first lover, suggest the difference between him and Kim. He was English-born, and had his heart set on a return to England. Kim, however, is deeply bound to India; he wants nothing more than to continue exploring its many roads. In a sense, he is already wed to the country, committed by his upbringing and his vocation to a life as a benevolent ruler of her people. His kiss seals this commitment, and symbolizes not only his inclusion but also that of his fellow country-born-and-bred Englishmen within the culture they are to rule.

For someone who has read through Kipling's Indian works, this episode is particularly moving and unexpected. It suggests that all along, as Kipling is praising his imperial heroes, depicting their sacrifices, exploring the weaknesses that make India hell for them, he is also thinking of how they fail their subjects, and looking for ways to mend this flaw as well as the others. Reference to the imperial breach of faith reemerges, perhaps for political reasons, only when Kipling has what he considers a solution to the problem, a mold that will form the ideal benevolent despot. Then, in an act of breathtaking inclusiveness, he reintroduces Lispeth and invites us to read Kim not alone, but in the context of all his Indian works—a history that ends in the achievement of social harmony.

NOTES

22. Rudyard Kipling, "Lispeth," in *Plain Tales*, p. 7.
23. Ibid., p. 8.

—John A. McClure, *Kipling and Conrad: The Colonial Fiction*
(Cambridge: Harvard University Press, 1981): pp. 50–51, 74–76.

JOHN MCBRATNEY ON KIPLING'S PORTRAYALS OF INTERRACIAL LOVE

[John McBratney is an Associate Professor of English at John Carroll University. In addition to the full-length study from which the following is excerpted, he has published several articles on Kipling and other Victorian authors. Here he deconstructs Kipling's "fiction of miscegenation."]

In his fiction about interracial love, Kipling revealed the same ambivalence about the hybrid as his Anglo-Indian contemporaries: a fascination with the transgressive allure of "miscegenation" combined with a profound fear of the instability brought about by racial mixture.[32] This fear might seem odd given the pleasure he took in portraying the mingling of Indian and British influences in the white creole. However, for him the fusion implicit in Indo-British love was different from the liminal exchange found in the native-born. Here, we must distinguish between mingling and mixture. Mingling denotes a combination of elements that preserves the integrity of the original components and permits them separate without change. Mixture, on the other hand, suggests the creation of a single, new entity that alters the integrity of the constituent elements. In Kipling, mingling describes a cultural phenomenon that allows for a variety of consequences, including reversal of the mingling process. In contrast, mixture (or fusion) describes primarily a biological event that limits variety by making reversal more problematic. Mingling is advantageous because it permits the kind of fluid ethnic self-fashioning, without loss of one's white identity, that Tods and Strickland for a while embody. Fusion, however, produces a disastrous, new form—the Eurasian—in which the "pure" Briton is irretrievably lost within the Indian.

Kipling's tales of miscegenation often involve both mingling and mixing. The beginning of these narratives often discloses a commingling of British and Indian elements in a "[l]ove [that] heeds not caste." While this love thrives, both the Indian woman and the British man can meet within a felicitous space between their cultures or retreat to their own societies without damaging repercussions. But at some point, this mingling threatens to produce a mixture from which the Briton cannot withdraw. For the Briton (since it is he rather than the Indian whom these tales finally concern), the most awkward embodiment of mixture is the Eurasian child, for he or she represents a biological fission in which the Briton is, in effect, irremediably submerged. But the Indian woman, as the potential mother of such a child, is ultimately just as frightening. In the end, for the Briton these two figures come to represent, in Kristeva's word, the "abject"—that alterior presence whom the Briton seeks to reject in order to define himself but who continually threatens to return, trespass the boundaries of his being, and destroy his autonomous selfhood.[33]

In the opposition between mingling and mixture, we can see two types of hybridity in Kipling: the metaphorical, cultural sort represented by the white creole and the literal, biological kind incarnated in the Eurasian. For Kipling, between these two there exists an uneasy divide: the former is welcome within his myth of the native-born; the latter is definitively barred. Indeed, it is against the latter that the former marks off the bounds of his own identity. We turn now to Kipling's writings about miscegenation, looking first at his narratives of Indo-British love and then at two concerning Eurasians.

It is no exaggeration to say that, in his Indian writings, Kipling was obsessed with the theme of interracial love. Five of the original forty short stories collected in *Plain Tales from the Hills* (1888)—"Lispeth," "'Yoked with an Unbeliever,'" "Kidnapped," "Beyond the Pale," and "To be Filed for Reference"—concern love or marriage between an Indian woman and a British man. Several tales, sketches, and poems from succeeding collections also touch upon this theme. In addition, two of his novels, *The Naulahka: A Story of West and East* (1892) and *Kim* (1901), feature potential, though quickly averted, interracial liaisons.[34]

In most of these works, Kipling's treatment of interracial love avoids real political, moral, and aesthetic risk. Two of these stories, "Lispeth" (1886) and "Georgie Porgie" (1888), feature indigenous heroines who pose no threat to British authority. Although both tales concern good, loving Indian women who suffer at the hands of callous British men, their protagonists— Lispeth, a hill woman, and Georgiana, a Burmese—belong to ethnic groups with whose members nonelite Britons might enjoy sexual relations without official disapproval. After the 1857 Rebellion (a revolt caused in part by the Indian sense that Britons were interfering in Indian domestic and religious life), the British Raj was wary of meddling in matters of custom. Sexual liaisons with women protected by purdah or governed by caste were liable to incite Indian social and religious feeling. Amours with hill tribal women (like Lispeth), who were free of purdah restrictions, or Burmese women (like Georgiana), who as Buddhists fell outside the caste system, were far less likely to inflame indigenous sentiments. The nonthreat posed by the women in these stories is mirrored by the innocuousness of their male counterparts. The wandering naturalist in "Lispeth" and the feckless, freelancing Georgie in "Georgie Porgie" have little impact on the routine functioning of the Raj. In tales in which both the male and female characters carry so little social and political import, the sympathy we feel for the two women is uncomplicated by any consideration of danger to British rule.

NOTES

32. For the origin of the term "miscegenation," see Young, 144–47.

33. Following Freud and Mary Douglas, Julia Kristeva defines abjection as a process both psychological and social by which the individual seeks a coherent sense of identity by excluding from his or her selfhood that which is deemed foreign. By abjection, or expelling, what society considers impure (improper substances, like menstrual blood or feces, or illicit sexual acts, like incest or masturbation), the individual creates a socially approved identity whose borders

are marked by what has been expelled. However, the abjected, "like an inescapable boomerang" (1), refuses to remain excluded. Instead, it haunts the individual as the forbidden that may return. Combining "condemnation and yearning" (10), abjection signifies that against which the self constitutes itself but toward which it moves, desirously, in contravention of social norms. Abjection is a condition of boundaries; in its liminality, it "is above all ambiguity" (9). The abject, Kristeva writes, is "something rejected from which one does not part" (4). On the relevance of Kristeva's theory to narratives of interracial love under colonialism, see McClintock, 71–74, 245–46, 270–73.

34. Nearly all Kipling's narratives of Indo-British love concern British men and Indian women. Only one story, "Wee Willie Winkee," entertains the possibility of sexual relations between the English female and the Indian male, hinted at in the abduction of Miss Allardyce by a band of Pathans. Kipling's reluctance to handle this theme contrasts with the eagerness of many post-1857 Anglo-Indian writers to take it on. Nancy Paxton notes the obsession of these authors with "the rape script"—the mythic (largely apocryphal) narrative featuring the pure Englishwoman as the object of male Indian lust. On the discourse of rape in British narratives during and after the Rebellion, see Paxton, 109–64; and Sharpe, 57–82.

> —John McBratney, *Imperial Subjects, Imperial Space: Rudyard Kipling's Fiction of the Native-Born* (Columbus: Ohio State University Press, 2002): pp. 63–65.

MARTIN SEYMOUR-SMITH ON KIPLING'S EARLY USE OF IRONY

[The late Martin Seymour-Smith was a British critic, biographer, poet, and author of more than forty books, including *The 100 Most Influential Books Ever Written*. In this extract from his biography of Kipling, Seymour-Smith analyzes the author's emergent technique.]

The first real stories Kipling wrote appeared in the *Civil and Military* from 1886 onwards. They were collected under the title *Plain Tales from the Hills* in 1888, and published by a firm in Bombay. They became very popular in India almost instantly, but the copies that went to England were for the time being almost unheeded there. Very naturally and properly, they are exceedingly journalistic. But that does not obscure their merit. Kay Robinson, seeing Kipling's talent, gave him the opportunity to write these sketches (which is what they really are) by inaugurating 'turnovers', 'column-and-a-quarters', tales which started on the front page and were then continued further into the paper. They contain much of the later Kipling in embryo. But there is little sign in them, as yet, of what may be called Kipling's 'mature imperialism', the kind of attitude just described. They are certainly brilliant, with some powerful descriptive prose in them. They are essentially hard and cynical little pieces, extraordinarily professional for so young a man, and often over-redolent with worldly wisdom. It is their professionalism, though, that distinguishes them as remarkable. The knowingness is smart. It is not often actually offensive, although it becomes monotonous. Yet his audience is being got at, their assumptions are being questioned. Any serious writer, even a comic one, must question assumptions in order to obtain the 'shock of recognition'. The degree of consciousness of Kipling's use of irony is a matter for speculation; but the irony is irresistibly present. 'Lisbeth', the first tale in the book, is specifically against the sort of Christianity practised amongst the Anglo-Indians, and, in its way, all 'for' primitive innocence and trust and love. But the attitude is strategically detached. The Hill-girl who has taken to Christianity and has not reverted to her own religion ('as do some Hill-girls') finds an injured Englishman. He flirts with her and then, on the advice of the wife of the chaplain who is her mistress, pretends to her that he will return and marry her. She has taken his attentions with the greatest possible seriousness. 'It takes a great deal of Christianity to wipe out uncivilised Eastern instincts, such as falling in love at first sight.' The Englishman does not return and the Hill-girl is then told by the chaplain's wife that she had been assured that he would do so only 'as an excuse to keep you quiet': Englishmen are of 'superior clay'. The patronising unkindness of this is all the more evident for being presented without comment.

Lisbeth now does revert: 'she took to her own unclean people savagely'. The moral is sharp and obvious. These people were liars and not Christians; they made light of her feelings. Whether the worth of Christianity itself is being questioned is not perfectly clear; but there is irony in the use of the word 'unclean'. Thus Kipling is being sharply critical of the Christianity practised by chaplains and their wives in India. And, by contrast, he is presenting the Hill-girl as full of faith: she cannot at first even comprehend how what the chaplain's wife told her could be a lie, such was her trust in the moral superiority of these people—whose actual moral superiority is of course thus called into question. The poignancy of her desertion, though, is kept right back, as is emotion in general: one only knows that the author feels it because it provides him with the vehicle of his satire, or at least of his irony.

Already, in this 'turnover' for his newspaper, Kipling has developed a strategy. Those who like to believe in 'love-at-first-sight' can rejoice with Kipling in his irony. Those who go unmoved by such notions need take no notice. But the youthful romantic message is obvious, even if it was in no way necessary to Kipling at this stage. It is not at all deeply felt—it might just be a value to which Kipling is appealing on behalf of anyone else out there who is young and romantic—but it is there. And when Anglo-Indians talked about Kipling in later years, it was as a young man 'with ideas above his station', even as 'subversive': the impression, one feels, that any writer worth his salt would have to create amongst such people. If Kipling was spying, he was spying for himself. Yet readers even as rigid in their assumptions as the Anglo-Indians do not mind individual exceptions to their rules, provided they have nice mainsprings like love-at-first-sight. Kipling knows what he can get away with. He displays his cunning from the very beginning.

—Martin Seymour-Smith, *Rudyard Kipling*, (London: Queen Anne Press, 1989): 69–70.

"The Church That Was at Antioch"

One of several tales Kipling set during the Roman Empire, "The Church that was at Antioch" is a theologically and historically dense foray into the early years of Christianity that resonated as much with Kipling's India as it does with modern times.

Valens is the young hero, a capable and dutiful Roman living on the Eastern fringe of the empire and a clear historical analog for the Anglo-Indian civil servants populating many of Kipling's contemporary stories. Strengthening the correlation is Valen's devotion to Mithraism, an Eastern-influenced mystery cult that presaged Freemasonry in its emphasis on communal brotherhood and civic service; its incorporation of degrees of initiation; its appeal to soldiers and bureaucrats; and its tolerant acceptance of all men of honor, regardless of race or social standing. Worried that his proximity to "free-thinking" Constantinople was undermining his Roman heritage, Valens' well-born mother uses her influence to have him transferred to Antioch, where his uncle Lucius Sergius is prefect of police.

Sergius, or "Serga" as he is more often called, is a practical man whose views on religion extend only to its impact on his ability to keep the peace. First-century Antioch, like colonial (and for that matter, modern-day) India, was a cauldron of religious factions forever threatening to boil over into violent conflict. A heated debate about proper food preparation for communal feasts has pitted Hebrew Christians against their upstart Greek brethren within a community led by one Gaius Julius Paulus, better known as St. Paul. Valens first encounters Paul when an unruly mob of Jews, hoping to get rid of the fiery apostle and make trouble for the Christians, tries to pin the blame for its assembly on him. Proving his seasoning, Valens recognizes the old trick, lets Paul go, and arrests one of the real conspirators. When Paul leaves Antioch to retrieve St. Peter in the hopes of quelling the unrest within the Church, another riot breaks out during a Christian "love-feast" (communal dinner) and a Cicilian rogue, whose brother Valens killed earlier during an ambush attempt, seizes the opportunity for revenge. Valens thwarts the assassin but, in an act of almost superhuman empathy, lets the man go when he learns of his motive.

Paul returns with Peter and both men are asked to meet with Serga to discuss their strategy for calming the situation down. The two Church leaders are portrayed as diametric opposites: Paul the virile and over-confident revolutionary and Peter a brooding shadow still wracked with guilt over his denial of Christ. Kipling uses this meeting, and the story as a whole, as an opportunity to critique the sort of dogmatic emphasis on commandments that all organized religions display in one way or another, but in a scene that is repeated at tale's end, he uses the Mithraist youth as his mouthpiece instead of the saints: "Gods do not make laws. They change men's hearts. The rest is Spirit."

Paul immediately recognizes the wisdom in Valens' words, proclaiming them "the utter Doctrine itself." He then launches into the story of Christ's incarnation and his own epiphany. Peter picks up the tale with his pivotal conversion of the Roman officer Cornelius and the resultant realization that everyone is fit to receive the Word, that in fact "there is nothing under heaven that we dare call unclean." Paul seizes on this statement as clear support of his own position on the future of the Church and there is a moment of tension between the two saints. This is followed by further debate on how to approach the conflict between Greek and Hebrew Christians. Peter suggests segregation but Paul asserts that will lead to a schism, something they must avoid at all costs. Recognizing his own sin of pride, and conceding Peter's greater rhetorical power, Paul stipulates that is should be Peter, the "Rock on which His Church should stand," who delivers the sermon. As they part, Paul is overcome by a bout of malaria. This seemingly inapposite episode actually serves to further humanize the saint, and pull a narrative rising quickly toward pure theological discourse back to earth, lest we forget that these are actual, historical men we are reading about, with all the ailments and mortal worries of their time.

The next day Peter addresses the Church; but instead of rioting, the congregation "talked about the new orders for their love-feasts, most of them agreeing that they were sensible and easy." Valens successfully disperses the crowd without incident and strolls with Peter and Paul to his uncle's house. On the way, a Jewish boy approaches and taunts them with a song deriding Christ. While the Roman lectors (guards) who accompany Valens are chasing off the boy, the Cicilian assassin once more capitalizes on a moment of distraction, leaping from the shadows and stabbing Valens. The young Roman is rushed to his uncle's house, where Serga vows revenge on the Cicilian and his co-conspirators, but Valens, with his dying breath, pleads for mercy on his murderers' behalf. "Don't be hard on them....They get worked up....They don't know what they are doing." Both apostles hear the echo of Christ's words on the cross. Paul suggests baptizing Valens on the spot but Peter, displaying a deeper understanding of Christ's teaching and finally assuming his true stature, decrees that Valens needs no imprimatur from them "to certify him to any God."

In this deft deconstruction of Christian doctrine, Kipling not only educates readers about the origins of the Church and the dangers of pride and dogma, he also promotes a more generalized understanding of how the virtues of sacrifice and forgiveness supersede all religious and racial divisions.

"The Church That Was at Antioch"

Valens is the young Roman newly transferred to Antioch to serve under his uncle, the prefect of police. A Mithraist, Valens takes pains to point out Christianity's borrowings from his religion and even becomes a Christ-figure in the end by pleading mercy for his murderer. Valens is paralleled elsewhere in Kipling's fiction by subalterns serving in India.

Lucius Serguis, a.k.a. **Serga**, is Valens' uncle and Antioch's prefect of police, charged with quelling the religious uprisings that afflict his city. A practical, fair-minded man given to phrases like "the same with men as horses" Serga's only objection to "fancy religions" is that "they mostly meet after dark, and that means more work for Police."

Gaius Julius Paulus is St. Paul (née Saul), the fiery apostle who the Jews try to set up as a troublemaker. Paul's greatest strengths are also his greatest weaknesses—pride and conviction. Though he convinces Peter to keep the Church united, Paul's narrow conception of spiritual worth is displayed by his desire to baptize and convert Valens at the end.

Petrus is St. Peter (née Simon), the brooding apostle still recovering from his betrayal of Jesus. Though he successfully settles the dispute over food preparation, Peter only assumes his true authority as "the Rock on which His Church should stand" at the very end when he rebukes Paul for his prideful suggestion that Valens needs their blessing to "certify him to any God."

"The Church That Was at Antioch"

PHILIP MASON ON THE THEME OF FORGIVENESS

[The late Philip Mason was a noted historian, Kipling
scholar, and author of *The Men Who Ruled India*, among
other works. In this extract from his biography of
Kipling, Mason identifies several supporting elements
that serve the story's main theme of forgiveness.]

It is hard to illustrate Kipling's beliefs because there are so many
facets and such a wealth of points that might be made. But one
story that displays a wider variety of themes than most is 'The
Church that was at Antioch' (1929). Valens is a young Roman
officer whose mother is disturbed by his adherence to the cult of
Mithras, and she therefore pulls strings in Rome to get him
transferred to Antioch, where his uncle is head of the police.
Valens and his uncle Sergius, like all Kipling's Romans, are very
English and have been, one feels, to a good public school;
Sergius is the wise old Commissioner, Valens the dedicated
young subaltern, eager to put the world to rights, very like the
Brushwood Boy except that he has a girl whom he had bought in
the market at Constantinople.

The two Romans look on Antioch much as a British officer in
India looked on Lucknow; you had to know something of the
difference between Sunni and Shi'a, as well as between Muslim
and Hindu, if you were to keep them from flaring up in riot and
cutting each other's throats. And Valens has to learn of the
quarrels between Jewish Christians and Greek, all the problems
of how far the old Jewish Law should be obeyed by new
Christian converts. There are troublemakers from Jerusalem
eager to pin something on the Christians that will discredit them
in Roman eyes. They find a Cilician with a grievance; Valens had
killed his brother, who attacked him in a mountain pass when he
was on his way to Antioch. They make an opportunity for this
Cilician to kill Valens at a Christian gathering, but the

bodyguard seize him in time and Valens lets him go when he hears of the brother, saying that now it is even-throws. Valens is a good officer, conscientious and sympathetic and only mildly contemptuous of the Christians because they have borrowed so much from Mithraism; both he and Sergius have a respect for Paul the local leader, and for that greater leader Peter, whom Paul brings from Jerusalem to settle their disputes. Peter thinks there might be advantage in having separate tables for those of Greek and Jewish origin; Paul will have none of it. Valens tells Paul that at the feasts in honour of Mithras they make no difference between peoples; 'we are all His children,' says Valens, and goes on when pressed: 'Men make laws, not Gods ... Gods do not make laws. They change men's hearts. The rest is the Spirit'—a saying that Paul excitedly claims as 'the utter Doctrine itself'.

So we have Valens and Paul each claiming the true doctrine and thinking the other has it in a borrowed or perverted form. And this theological exchange is set against a counterpoint between the politico-religious disputes—which have really nothing to do with religion—and the Roman determination to keep the peace; with them it is part of the technique of good government to keep the crowds moving, to steer them homeward at the right moment. Then develops a new theme, the contrast between Paul—voluble, well-educated, highly articulate, utterly dedicated—and Peter. Paul is clear that there can be only one answer to the question of Greek and Jew; no compromise is possible; God has made all men equal in the spirit. But Peter is dumb—a great clumsy man, whose right hand has withered since he raised it to deny his Master, and he is still obsessed with the memory of that denial. He is inconsistent, infirm of purpose; he has to be pushed and primed by Paul until he is brought to the point. Then at last he speaks with a force Paul cannot match and carries the day.

There is a minor theme, the girl Valens had bought; she does not have much to say before the finale, but she comes like an unaccompanied phrase on a flute, a few simple notes that we know will recur. When Paul is struck down with fever, she brings a cloak of jackal-skins to warm him and, later, when the

Christians have gone, she asks about Peter. Valens tells her that he believes he once denied his God.

> She halted in the moonlight, the glossy jackal skins over her arm.
> 'Does he? My God bought me from the dealers like a horse. Too much, too, he paid. Didn't he? 'Fess, thou?'

She stands for a moment, alive, laughing and adoring; the glossy jackal-skins in the moonlight bring her sharp to the eye.

Next day was the great meeting when Peter spoke; he won the day, the Romans gently dispersed the crowds to their homes. Paul and Peter relaxed, 'now that the day's burden is lifted,' and Valens asks them to his uncle's house. As they stroll there, an impudent boy lures the bodyguard away and an assassin runs in to stab Valens under the ribs. It was the same Cilician whom he had spared before. As he lies dying, Valens begs his uncle: 'Don't be too hard on them ... They get worked up ... They don't know what they are doing ... Promise!' Peter and Paul recognize the Word from the Cross and Paul suggests that they should baptize the dying Roman.

> Painfully, that other raised the palsied hand that he had once held up ... to deny a charge.
> 'Quiet!' said he. 'Think you that one who has spoken Those Words needs such as *we* are to certify him to any God?'
> Paul cowered before the unknown colleague, vast and commanding, revealed after all these years.

In the closing bars, the minor theme is heard again. The girl has been trying to warm Valens with the furs and with the warmth of her body. Now 'the brow beneath her lips was chilling, even as she called on her God who had bought her at a price that he should not die but live.'

All the themes of the story thus meet in the finale. It proclaims as a supreme virtue the forgiveness of wrong, planned and carried out deliberately, but in the same breath it denies that this virtue is exclusively Christian. But, as in the verses 'Cold Iron' and in 'The Gardener', it uses Christian symbols without hesitation.

> —Philip Mason, *Kipling: The Glass, the Shadow and the Fire*, (London: Jonathon Cape, 1975): pp. 253–256.

ANGUS WILSON ON KIPLING'S HUMANIST CHRISTIANITY

[In another extract from his Kipling biography, Wilson explains how the story offers a rare, unadulterated glimpse of the author's personal views on spirituality.]

"The Church That Was at Antioch" is a delight to read. The young Roman patrician, Valens, who is posted to the police service at Antioch, is presented to us with the same affection as Parnesius on the Roman Wall or District Commissioner Orde on the Frontier; and we are equally prepared to believe that he deserves it. But whereas Parnesius and Orde learn the nature of men and how to govern them in savage outposts, Valens learns in the intrigues and hatreds of a crowded city life. The Jewish Christians and the Gentile Christians (Paul's converts) of Antioch are in dispute over the eating of forbidden foods at the Passover feasts. The orthodox Jews of the city are looking for and seeking to use any disturbances that may come out of the Christian deliberations, as a cause of civil complaint against the Christians to Valens's uncle, Lucius Sergius, head of the Antioch police.

Kipling is at his story-telling best here. There are no frames (either the over-complicated kind of his later work or the brash "I" voice of his early work). Valens has only a few days—a week perhaps—in which to learn how to administer justice decently, for at the very moment when he has proved himself he is killed by an assassin's dagger. The short life is well chosen for the short story. In 25 pages we are convinced both by Valens's political action and by the spiritual growth that accompanies it. And—no easy task—Kipling maintains all the time behind this individual story the sense of the teeming, tense city all the time on the verge of mob rule. But, as if this were not enough, Kipling dares to introduce the figures of St Paul and St Peter, who have come to decide the point at dispute in the Christian quarrel over the feast ritual. His success is complete. Both are absolutely convincing figures as much in their extraordinary outward appearance, as in their widely different modes of thought and feeling.

There is little comfort in this story for those who would claim Kipling in his later years for orthodox Christianity. As far as the world goes, Valens preaches the gospel of duty to the civil law from everyone and the unconcern of the civil law with a man's religious thoughts and practices where they do not break the law. It is the creed of Gallio when St Paul was brought before him at Achaia in the Acts of the Apostles and it is one of Kipling's favourite texts. As early as "The Judgement of Dungara", the Assistant Collector of the Berbula Hills is called Gallio and says to the Lutheran missionary—"Neigh ho! I have their bodies and the District to see to, but you can try what you can do for their souls. Only don't behave as your predecessor did, or I'm afraid that I cannot guarantee your life." It is Parnesius's declared civil creed on the Roman Wall. The story, "Little Foxes" (1909) of Adam Strickland's administration in East Africa is followed by the poem, "Gallio's Song":

> Whether ye rise for the sake of a creed,
> Or riot in hope of spoil,
> Equally will I punish the deed,
> Equally check the broil;
> Nowise permitting injustice at all
> From whatever doctrine it springs—
> But—whether ye follow Priapus or Paul,
> I care for none of these things.

It is reiterated by St Paul in the late twin story to "The Church That Was at Antioch", which tells of the lasting psychological (and spiritual) effect of Paul upon the captain of the ship in which he was wrecked on Malta—"The Manner of Men" (1930).

But "The Church That Was at Antioch" does not stop at this simple message, inheritance of the staple of British rule in India, it goes further into the nature of man's spiritual life. Valens is a

Mithraist, and he sees in Christianity many of the rituals and symbols that make his private military religion a comforting discipline. Parnesius had come near to making the same identification. I do not think that this approval of some aspects of Christianity via Mithraism suggests any strong religious belief in Kipling. He sees Mithraism as a sort of Freemasonry, a fellowship and ritual bound by a Deistic hope rather than any transcendent certainty. It is the feasting of the Christians in fellowship that awakens Valens's sympathy.

But there is a further dimension which marks Kipling's latest work. When Valens dies from the assassin's dagger, he tells his uncle, the Prefect of Police, "Don't be hard on them [those responsible for his murder] ... They get worked up ... They don't know what they are doing ... Promise!" The uncle answers, "This is not I, child. It is the Law." "No odds ... Men make laws not Gods." In short, Kipling now asks that mercy should transcend Gallio's administration. And the story now takes us deeper, for St Peter recognises Valens's words as a reflection of Christ's, "Forgive them for they know not what they do." Yet the idea of Christian salvation as such is rejected, for Paul wishes to baptise the dying Valens, but Peter scornfully rejects this "Think you that one who has spoken these words needs such as *we* are to certify him to any God?" And the following poem specifically rejects any doctrinal claim to supremacy:

> He that hath a Gospel
> Whereby Heaven is won
> (Carpenter or Cameleer,
> Or Maya's dreaming son),
> Many swords shall pierce Him
> Mingling blood with gall;
> But His Own Disciple
> Shall wound him worst of all![30]

Again and again Kipling uses the Christian texts and doctrines familiar to his readers, deeply imbued with his own family background, but they are seldom employed for purposes that cannot be explained either by humanist ethics or by spiritual search. Only once in the poem, "Cold Iron", that accompanies a story in *Rewards and Fairies*, does he seem to lay emphasis on any basic Christian doctrine—and here I think he uses the Crucifixion as a symbol for sacrifice and atonement, which were already beginning to play an important part in his general ethical creed and were to dominate stories like "The Wish House" ten years later.

But Jesus's plea for forgiveness of his enemies is certainly a central point of his later thinking. His son John's death surely turned him to this, for it first becomes central in "On the Gate", a tale of 1916. But the same allegory of judgement of souls is repeated in "Uncovenanted Mercies" (1932). The earlier story is cast in a witty-serious satire upon bureaucracy; the later one, making the Judgement Seat a railway station, is more a satire upon what we should now call social workers. Neither is unentertaining, although the flow of epigram and paradox has for me something of the irritating effect of that of a famous man of letters of the age who met Kipling only once to shake hands with him at Barrie's funeral—Bernard Shaw. And the plea for compassion is so general that it comes close all the time to sentimentality.

But it is certainly not so in "The Church That Was at Antioch" and Peter's rebuke of the narrowly doctrinal Paul is one of the best moments in Kipling. Yet, in the long run, Paul was very close to Kipling's heart as we may see in the poem that follows the story of Paul's shipwreck, "The Manner of Men". The words of "At His Execution", where St Paul makes his dying plea, have been seen by many critics to be that rare thing in Kipling's work—a revelation of himself.

> I was made all things to all men,
> But now my course is done—
> And now is my reward—
> Ah, Christ, when I stand at Thy Throne
> With those I have drawn to the Lord,
> Restore me to my self again!

NOTE

30. "The Disciple"

—Angus Wilson, *The Strange Ride of Rudyard Kipling* (New York: Viking, 1978): pp. 337–340.

JAMES HARRISON ON IDEALIZED YOUTH

[Here Harrison find parallels (and highlights the key differences) between Valens and the Anglo-Indian subalterns that Kipling champions elsewhere in his fiction.]

More compelling in many ways [than "The Manner of Men"] is "The Church that Was at Antioch," in which both St. Paul and St. Peter are upstaged by a young Roman police officer named Valens. Even more than Parnesius, Valens recalls those idealized young heroes of the early stories. He "has all the firmness, tact and tolerance which a first-class English subaltern might be expected to show in face of some more or less incomprehensible communal squabble in British India."[5] For the Syria where he finds himself posted to serve under his uncle, Sergius, is presented as uncannily like India under British rule. Substitute, for Hindus and Moslems, Christians of Jewish and Christians of Gentile extraction, engaged in bitter strife (fanned by agents from the synagogue in Jerusalem) over such matters as what food is ceremonially fit to be eaten. Under his uncle's wise tutelage, however, he soon becomes a shrewd judge of situations. The tone of the story verges, at times, on the complacent arrogance of the Anglo-Indian, yet is miraculously rescued by Valens himself, who is never quite too good to be true. (Perhaps the fact that he owns a young slave girl rescues him from the self-righteousness of a Bobby Wicks or a Brushwood Boy.)

Paul has gone in search of Peter to help resolve the food disputes, and in his absence Valens narrowly escapes death while calming an artificially provoked riot. He lets his would-be murderer escape, however, so as not to bring further trouble on the harassed Christians. Finally, after Paul and a moodily self-doubting Peter have restored peace to their congregation, Valens is stabbed in a dark alley and dies pleading with his uncle, "Don't be hard on them.... They get worked up.... They don't know what they are doing" (33:121).

The whole story is in fact full of references to the crucifixion. Sergius, in refusing to arrest Paul just because the Jews want him to, adds that "One of our Governors tried that game down-coast—for the sake of peace—some years ago. He didn't get it" (100). Peter, unsure of himself throughout the story, turns on Paul at one point to ask, "Do you too twit me with my accent?" (109). Valens's slave girl refers to him, more than once, as "her God who had bought her at a price" (122). Valens impresses Paul early in the story, moreover, by the way he can penetrate through all the superficialities of religion to the heart of the matter. "But—as a servant of Mithras, shall we say—how think you about our food-disputes?" Paul asks him.

> "As a servant of Mithras I eat with any initiate, so long as the food is clean," said Valens.
> "But," said Petrus, "that is the crux."
> "Mithras also tells us," Valens went on, "to share a bone covered with dirt, if better cannot be found."
> "You observe no difference, then, between peoples at your feasts?" Paulus demanded.
> "How dare we? We are all His children. Men make laws. Not Gods," Valens quoted from the old Ritual.
> "Say that again, child!"
> "Gods do not make laws. They change men's hearts. The rest is the Spirit."
> "You heard it, Petrus? You heard that? It is the utter Doctrine itself!" (33:107–108)

But it is Peter who responds, in awe, to the dying words already quoted. "'Forgive them, for they know not what they do.' Heard you *that*, Paulus? He, a heathen and an idolator, said it." Quick to agree, Paul adds, "What hinders now that we should baptize him?" But he has no answer when Peter, finding the authority which has eluded him up to this point, asks quietly, "Think you that one who has spoken Those Words needs such as *we* are to certify him to any God?" (122.)

The story is far from a pious Christian tract. Indeed, Mithraism comes out of it rather better than Christianity, as does Masonry, that other simple soldiers' creed, in other stories. And Valens is more than a match for the two saints. Moreover, Peter's final words express something very close to Kipling's own views on the merits of this form of religion as opposed to that one. The source of the values embodied in the story is much more clearly that line of self-sacrificial devotion to duty one can trace in Kipling's early stories about idealized subalterns and selfless administrators, right on through Parnesius and Pertinax in *Puck of Pook's Hill*, and which here reaches its apotheosis—the man of action who is peacemaker and savior. To have written once more of the self-sacrificial heroism of the British subaltern—of the post-1914 subalterns dying by the thousands in a blood bath to which Kipling must sometimes have felt he had dispatched his only son—would have cut too near the bone. By transposing such heroism to Syria in the first century, however, Kipling can reaffirm, with a deepened understanding of the nature of the task and of the price demanded, all his earlier faith in youth.

NOTE

5. J.I.M. Stewart, *Rudyard Kipling* (New York, 1966), p. 202.

—James Harrison, *Rudyard Kipling* (Boston: Twayne, 1982): pp. 112–114.

SANDRA KEMP ON THE PROBLEMS OF DISCIPLESHIP

[Sandra Kemp is Director of Research at the Royal College of Art (UK) and the author and/or editor of numerous books, including *Feminisms* and *The Oxford Companion to Edwardian Fiction: 1900–1914.* In this extract from her book on Kipling, Kemp assesses the story's critique of discipleship.]

'The Church that was at Antioch' picks up and develops the theme of the problems of discipleship already hinted at in 'The Manner of Men'. The story's epigraph is taken from Galatians 2.11—'But when Peter was come to Antioch, I withstood him to the face, because he was to blame'—and refers to the arguments of the early Church over whether Jews and Gentiles should eat at the same table. The concluding poem, 'The Disciple', contains a warning to Peter, Paul and all 'disciples' that every disciple has his limitations of vision and his own personality is a potential threat to truth. There is an obvious analogy with the chameleon ambivalence of the artist:

> It is His Disciple
>   (Ere Those Bones are dust)
> Who shall change the Charter,
>   Who shall split the Trust—
> Amplify distinctions,
>   Rationalise the Claim,
> Preaching that the Master
>   Would have done the same
>
>   . . . . .
>
> He that hath a Gospel
>   Whereby Heaven is won
> (Carpenter, or Cameleer,
>   Or Maya's dreaming son),
> Many swords shall pierce Him,
>   Mingling blood with gall;
> But His Own Disciple
>   Shall wound Him worst of all!

In this story the contrast between Peter's brooding nature and Paul's energetic and articulate vision is very powerful. Paul is presented sympathetically as a radical thinker who is struggling to understand Christ's vision, to live in accordance with and to guide the early Church. His first conversation with Valens reveals that he has not yet mastered his pride:

> 'I expect you march in heavier order than I.'
> 'What would you call your best day's work?' Valens asked in turn.
> 'I have covered ...' Paulus checked himself. 'And yet not I but the God,' he muttered. 'It's hard to cure oneself of boasting.'

But, appropriately for the Paul of Acts and Galatians, who strove to free Christianity from the constraints of the Law, he is more immediately sympathetic than Peter to the claims of 'spirit' over 'law', and can respond at once to what Valens says about God changing men's hearts rather than making laws:

> 'As a servant of Mithras, I eat with any initiate, so long as the food is clean,' said Valens.
> 'But,' said Petrus, '*that* is the crux.'
> 'Mithras also tells us,' Valens went on, 'to share a bone covered with dirt, if better cannot be found.'
> 'You observe no difference, then, between peoples at your feasts?' Paulus demanded.
> 'How dare we? We are all his children. Men make laws. Not Gods,' Valens quoted from the Old Ritual ... 'Gods do not make laws. They change men's hearts. The rest is the Spirit.'

Peter, on the other hand, is uncertain about the food laws: 'It is true that I have eaten with Gentiles—Yet, at the time, I doubted if it were wise.' But it is he, not Paul, who intuitively realizes that there is no need to baptise Valens as he lies dying: 'Think you that one who has spoken Those Words needs such as *we* to certify him to any God?' His belief that this would be merely convention, set alongside the references to Mithraism in the story and to 'Maya's dreaming son' in the accompanying poem, suggests that Kipling retained his conviction that no single religion has the monopoly of truth. The conversation of Valens with his uncle at the beginning of the story restates his belief that there are the same archetypes within different religions, called by different names, and that the same basic patterns underlie all doctrine and religious observance:

> 'We've a College here of stiff-necked Hebrews who call themselves Christians.'
>
> 'I've heard of them,' said Valens. 'There isn't a ceremony or symbol they haven't stolen from the Mithras ritual.'
>
> 'Even these Christians are divided now. You see ... one part of their worship is to eat together.'
>
> 'Another theft! The Supper is the essential Symbol with us,' Valens interrupted.

At the end of the story Valens himself can be seen as a Christ figure. Stabbed to death in a dark alley by a coward who uses a child as a decoy, Valens repeatedly begs mercy for his murderers. His words recall those of the dying Christ on the cross: 'The Cilician and his friends ... Don't be hard on them ... They get worked up ... They don't know what they are doing'. Here too the references to his 'concubine' recall Christ's love and compassion for Mary Magdalene. In this context, however, the language suggests that a sacrificial human love is divine, if anything is, and that the one is best understood in terms of the other. At the same time, there is no easy interchange between the human and the supernatural in the story. In a final narrative twist, Peter and Paul are seen to be subservient to Valens, they are not the 'heroes' of this story, but only disciples after all.

—Sandra Kemp, *Kipling's Hidden Narratives* (Oxford: Basil Blackwell, 1988): pp. 97–99.

PLOT SUMMARY OF

"Mrs. Bathurst"

With the possible exception of "The Man Who Would Be King," no single work of fiction by Kipling has generated as much comment and criticism as "Mrs. Bathurst." Early reviewers, unaccustomed to the rigors of "experimental" fiction, considered it willfully unintelligible at worst, and at best an example of how Kipling let his zeal for revision get the best of him. Noted Kipling commentator C.A. Bodelsen dubbed it "the hardest of all the stories," an assessment that has been oft repeated ever since. While it is true that "Mrs. Bathurst" presents unique challenges, its purported opacity is, in fact, a reflection of an ingenious narrative technique many years ahead of its time that creates the opportunity for a truly interactive reading experience.

The facts of the frame story are not overly difficult to determine. Four men gather by chance in a railway siding in South Africa and pass the time drinking beer and reminiscing about several acquaintances, only two of which—a New Zealand innkeeper named Mrs. Bathurst and a naval warrant officer named Vickery—have anything more than a thematic relationship to each other, and even that is left highly ambiguous. Dialogue is rendered naturally, that is to say without any rhetorical interference that would steer it in the direction of a "story," per se. The overall effect on the reader is of eavesdropping on an interesting conversation in which *something* is communicated, but one can't say for certain exactly what. In order to make any sense out of it at all, ultimately readers must, as it were, *tell themselves* the story. Fortunately, and contrary to early opinion, every detail in the story can help guide readers on their way.

Perhaps the best way to tackle the inner narrative is to first determine what can be conclusively deduced, and then fill the gaps with educated guesswork. From Pyecroft we learn that Vickery became so obsessed with a reel of "documentary" film showing Mrs. Bathurst getting off a train at a London station that he revisited the fair where it was shown for five consecutive nights and each time compelled Pyecroft to join him, following the screenings, in all-night drinking binges and manic ramblings about town. At one point Pyecroft finally confronts him and Vickery says two telling things. The first is that Mrs. Bathurst was looking for him that day in the station. The second, which comes a few days later, apropos of nothing, is that Vickery cannot be held responsible for his wife's death, because she died six weeks after he shipped out. "That much at least I am clear of." Pyecroft also tells us that shortly after these episodes Vickery was sent into the interior on a solo ammunition-delivery assignment, which he completed, after which promptly disappeared, risking court martial despite having only eighteen months of duty left. From Hooper we hear of the discovery of two lightning-charred corpses at a railway siding in the general vicinity of Vickery's last know whereabouts, one of which bore tattoos like Vickery's. Though he never reveals them, Hooper is also clearly carrying Vickery's false teeth in his pocket.

So, clearly, the two main mysteries of the story are what happened between Vickery and Mrs. Bathurst and what is the identity of the second tramp. Neither can be answered with any certainty, but there are just enough context clues to develop one of three possible theories. The most obvious possibility is that Mrs. Bathurst is the second tramp and that the two lovers were reunited in death. Textually, this can be supported by Hooper's (albeit ambiguous) use of the word "mate," by Pritchard's reaction to hearing about the corpses ("And to think of her at Hauraki!" he says, covering his eyes "like a child shutting out an ugliness."), and by an ironic reading of the concluding lines of the song sung by the picnickers ("Underneath the bower, 'mid the perfume and flower, / Sat a maiden with the one she loves the best—"). It has also been argued that Kipling was too deliberate a writer to introduce a new and otherwise functionless character at the very end of a story, so the second tramp *must* be Mrs. Bathurst. Even more tenuously, some have gone so far as to interpret a female shape in the illustration depicting the corpses that accompanied the story's original 1904 publication.

However compelling and poetically apt, the above theory is

far from ironclad. From a purely practical standpoint it is very unlikely that a Victorian woman would or even could travel alone from New Zealand to South Africa, disguise herself as a tramp, and somehow locate Vickery in the interior. Then there is the rather conspicuous fact that Hooper does not specify the sex of the second tramp, something he almost certainly would have done had it been a woman. More damning than these subjective quibbles is the story's overwhelming emphasis on the themes of disingenuousness and desertion. From the frame story's setting of "False Bay," to the Boy Niven and Moon episodes, to Pyecroft's playful jabs at Pritchard about his past dalliances, "Mrs. Bathurst" is full of subtle references to acts of infidelity, misdirection, and abandonment. More overt, but no less compelling, are Vickery's false teeth and "foul anchor" tattoo.

The last obstacle to Mrs. Bathurst's presence in the teak forest is the likelihood that she is *already dead*. As C.A. Bodelsen and several subsequent commentators have pointed out, the best explanation for why Vickery is *so* haunted by her appearance on the cinematograph is because he is looking at a dead woman, one for whose death he was in all likelihood at least indirectly responsible. The implicit suggestion is that she either discovered Vickery was already married or was simply "stood up" in London, and then died from her own hand or a broken heart. Textual support for her death is necessarily more elusive, lest Kipling preclude the beguiling possibility of her being the second tramp. Nevertheless, the highly nuanced wording of Vickery's non sequitur alibi for his "lawful" wife's death goes a long way towards situating Mrs. Bathurst in the afterlife.

So if Mrs. Bathurst is already dead, who is the second tramp? Some have argued that, far from being functionless, an anonymous second tramp perfectly serves the story's themes of misdirection and ambiguity. Others argue that, regardless of identity, the second tramp's crouched position and shielding gesture, when contrasted with Vickery's standing posture, indicates Vickery welcomed his death and rose to greet it. At least some support for a death wish in Vickery can be found in his response to Pyecroft's counter-threat of murder: "I'm almost afraid that 'ud be a temptation."

The last and most problematic solution to the mystery of the second tramp, and the one posited by Bodelsen, is that Mrs. Bathhurst is somehow both already dead *and* the second tramp. To accept this, we must envision a supernatural ending, bounded only by the limits of one's imagination and spiritual beliefs. As such, an examination of its merits hardly lies within the scope of the present work.

Needless to say, in attempting to pin down the story's two main mysteries, we have just scratched the surface of the many allusions and rhetorical clues that Kipling planted for his readers. The mythological and literary references, for example, have been left totally untouched, as has the relevance of the prefacing "Irenius" excerpt. For a thorough examination of both, plus an excellent summary of past scholarship on the story, see chapter four of Nora Crook's *Kipling's Myths of Love and Death*.

LIST OF CHARACTERS IN

"Mrs. Bathurst"

Hooper is the railway inspector who discovers the lightning-charred corpses in the teak forest and refrains, out of respect, from displaying Vickery's false teeth. Though Hooper never specifies the sex of the second tramp, some interpret his use of the word "mate" as proof that it was Mrs. Bathurst.

Pyecroft is the naval petty officer who accompanies Vickery to repeat viewings of the film reel showing Mrs. Bathurst getting off a train in London, and afterwards joins him in all-night drinking binges and rambles about town. Worried about Vickery's sanity, Pyecroft reports him to their commanding officer, who promptly assigns Vickery a solo mission into the interior.

Pritchard is the big sergeant of marines who arrives with Pyecroft at the railway siding where they encounter Hooper and the narrator. Pritchard's apparent affection for Mrs. Bathurst, at least partly based on her willingness to set aside and remember his favorite beer between visits, leave him most affected by the possibility of her death.

The narrator is exactly that—a nameless navy man of unspecified rank who faithfully reports the conversation but is unable to clarify, contextualize, or contribute any essential details of the story.

"Click" Vickery is the naval warrant officer haunted by the appearance of Mrs. Bathurst on the cinematograph. Clearly guilty of something, he eventually goes mad, deserts the navy, and is struck down by lightning.

Mrs. Bathurst is the proprietress of a hotel in New Zealand, a woman who "never scrupled to feed a lame duck or set 'er foot on a scorpion." Mrs. Bathurst has an affair of an unspecified nature with Vickery and is last seen in the film reel getting off a train in a London station.

"Mrs. Bathurst"

J.M.S. TOMPKINS ON KIPLING'S EXPERIMENTS IN SUPPRESSED NARRATIVE

[In this extract from her book on Kipling, Tompkins postulates a motive and a method behind the story's allusive incompleteness.]

In *Something of Myself* Kipling says that what is deleted must have been honestly written for inclusion first, and in his last story, 'Proofs of Holy Writ', he shows us Shakespeare telling his stubborn old friend, Ben Jonson, that he ought to have removed cartloads from his plays. The assumption is that what has once been honestly written will leave its traces, and that the tale—or the play—will benefit from it. If what is explicit is fully explored, if the dialogue, in particular, is read with a full participation of the imagination, it will be enriched by what the author has suppressed, as we feel the personality of an acquaintance without knowing all that went to shape it.

One of the earliest and most extreme of the experiments in suppressed narrative was 'Mrs Bathurst'. It is unlike the later experiments, such as 'Dayspring Mishandled', in two ways. There is no difficulty about its theme, which is the destroying power of love; on the other hand, no analysis can establish with certainty how the destruction came about. We see the gaunt shrine and the shrivelled victims, but we cannot trace the avenues of approach. If Kipling meant us to do so, it may be held, as Professor C. S. Lewis has suggested, that he has overdone his demolitions. But he may have meant the unexplained in the action to reflect the inexplicable in the theme. How and why does a candid, generous woman, who 'never scrupled to feed a lame duck or set 'er foot on a scorpion', become the vessel of a destructive power? If we were allowed to trace too closely the stages by which Vickery is destroyed, we might make the mistake of thinking that we know. So Vickery appears in Pyecroft's 'résumé' only in the last stages of his obsession, in Cape Town, and Mrs Bathurst is seen far off in Sergeant Pritchard's memories of New Zealand or momentarily on the screen of the early biograph, 'lookin' for 'somebody'. 'I'm trying to say solely what transpired', Pyecroft remarks; but 'what transpired' is more than the few facts he has to recount, because the men who tell and hear have knowledge of Aphrodite. Pyecroft knows that 'it takes 'em at all ages', and mentions his shipmate, Moon, who ran after sixteen years' service. Inspector Hooper knows that 'if a man gets struck with that kind of woman ... he goes crazy—or just saves himself', as he, perhaps, has done. The arid shore, the parching wind, the 'seven-coloured sea' of the setting are the fit haunt of the goddess, as the grotesque lightning-charred group in the teak-forest is a fit monument to her. Even the song of the casual picnic party and Pritch's involuntary irresistibility to servant-girls point in the same direction. 'I used to think seein' and hearin' was the only regulation aids to ascertainin' facts', says Pyecroft, 'but as we get older we get more accommodatin'. The cylinders work easier, I suppose.' Still, 'Mrs Bathurst' is hard on the cylinders.[1]

NOTE

1 The facts about Vickery are that he has a fifteen-year old daughter; his wife died in childbed six weeks after he came out, so that he is free; he did not murder her: there was 'a good deal between' him and Mrs Bathurst and he has some wrong or deceit against her on his mind. He says that she was looking for him at Paddington. He sees his Captain, is sent up-country alone and deserts eighteen months before his pension is due. He is found dead with a woman after a thunderstorm. Pyecroft and Pritchard both insist that it was not Mrs Bathurst's fault. She was left a widow very young, never remarried, and had the respect of the non-commissioned and warrant officers who went to her little hotel in Hauraki. The scene *From Lyden's 'Irenius'* that precedes the tale makes the point that the groom, or clown, is caught in the same noose as kings—this may account for the grotesque stress on 'Click'; that the woman destroyed him in ignorance, for she loved him; and that the groom in the end threw life from him out of weariness and self-disgust—which suggests that Vickery stood up to attract the lightning. This is not a continuous narrative; but neither is it confusion. Rather it is like the early biograph, 'just like life ... only when any one came down too far towards us that was watchin', they walked right out of the picture, so to speak'.

—J.M.S. Tompkins, *The Art of Rudyard Kipling* (London: Methuen, 1959): pp. 89–90.

C.A. BODELSEN ON THE CENTRALITY OF THE CINEMATOGRAPH

[C.A. Bodelsen was a Professor of English Language and Literature at the University of Copenhagen and the author of numerous works, including *Aspects of Kipling's Art*. The following extract focuses on Kipling's early and ingenious use of film as a potent psychological device.]

I am convinced that in order to find the meaning of *Mrs Bathurst* one must start from the film episode. If its full implications are realized, it comes out as the most original and striking idea of the tale. It contains most of the information necessary for an understanding of the latter, and I should not be surprised to learn that for Kipling it was the point round which he built the whole story.

It is easy to miss something here, because after sixty years we have most of us ceased to feel that there is anything very wonderful in the fact that a film can show us people at the other end of the world, or even people who are not in the world any more. I shall come back to the latter point, but for the moment I would stress that this cannot have been the way people felt about the cinema in 1904. To them, its possibilities must have seemed little short of marvellous, and in this story we see Kipling, with his usual originality, seizing on this and working out its implications for his own art, as he did with another new invention in *Wireless*.

I spoke above of the information about the characters of the story that can be gleaned from its film motif. This information is: that Mrs Bathurst has left New Zealand for London (this must be fairly recently, as Pyecroft says the episode of the beer bottles was 'in 1901, mark you'. Further that she is looking for Vickery. Besides serving a symbolical purpose (to which I shall return below), I believe that this must be taken quite literally: she has come to London to find him. One notes that the picture shows her arriving at Paddington Station by the Western Mail Train. Such details often convey something of importance in Kipling; in this case it tells us that she has just landed in one of the western ports.

And furthermore, if one reads Pyecroft's description of the film carefully, it tells us something of the utmost importance for the understanding of the story; it gives us the missing piece that makes the jigsaw puzzle come out as a meaningful picture, viz. that *Mrs Bathurst* is dead when Vickery and Pyecroft see her on the screen.

When one's attention has been called to this by the description of the picture, one even realizes that it can be deduced from the facts we already know from the story. For we have been pointedly told that Vickery's wife has recently died in childbed, and that he has only a short time to wait before he is pensioned off, when there would be nothing to prevent him from going to New Zealand or London or wherever Mrs Bathurst might be. This information must be meant to tell us that he is now a free man. (Kipling calls attention to this by making Pyecroft say: 'if what 'e said about 'is wife was true he was a free man as 'e stood'.) There would then be nothing to prevent him from marrying Mrs Bathurst, *if she were still alive*, in which case the wrong he did her would presumably be expiated, and their love affair brought to a quite prosaic conclusion. There would be no need for him to torture himself by seeing her picture every night, nor for their death in the thunderstorm.

But apart from the above, the description of Vickery and Pyecroft at the cinema show contains two indications that it is a dead woman they see on the screen. The first is Vickery's reaction to the sight, which is that of a haunted man. But it is also indicated symbolically—and I think unmistakably—in the account of the film itself. In this we are first told that 'when anyone came down too far towards us that was watchin' they walked out of the picture, so to speak'. If this were meant merely as a piece of description, there is no need that it should be repeated. In fact, it is hardly an exaggeration to say that there are no gratuitous repetitions in the stories in Kipling's late manner. But it is repeated some ten lines further down, and amplified in a way that, according to his usual practice of indirect communication, seems to mean something: when Mrs Bathurst appears among the crowd coming out of the train, Pyecroft says: 'She walked on and on till she melted out of the picture—like—

like a shadow jumpin' over a candle.' (The word 'shadow', with its significant overtones, and also 'candle' ('the candle of life') again look like verbal pointers.)

And by telling us that Mrs Bathurst is dead, the film motif also gives us the clue to one of the other enigmas of the story: what was the sin that Vickery had committed? Clearly, it had some connection with her. What then was the meaning of his confidence to Pyecroft: 'I am not a murderer, because my lawful wife died in childbed six weeks after I came out. That much at least I am clear of.'

For one thing, of course, he is telling Pyecroft that he has an alibi as far as his wife's death is concerned. But it also tells us other things. Why this insistence on his alibi for his wife's death, when there is no mention that anybody thought he had been guilty of it? It looks as if he had been tempted to do away with her, though he did not do so, and for what other purpose than to marry another woman? (In 1904, and even today, it would have been impossible for him to get a divorce.)

But the most important fact it conveys to us is that until he came out to South Africa he maintained marital relations with his wife, and that she was expecting a baby when Mrs Bathurst came to London to find him. And this would, for a respectable man like Vickery, be a valid reason—or excuse—to tell her he could not leave his wife for her.

'I am not a murderer.' But a man who causes the death of a woman by driving her to take her own life or to die of a broken heart is not technically a murderer, though his guilt may be as heavy as if he were. And this I believe is what Vickery did. I think the clues we have examined put us in a position to answer the question: what was Vickery's guilt, and what happened to Mrs Bathurst after the story left her at her hotel at Hauraki?

The following is an attempt to make explicit what Kipling expected us to guess from the clues he planted in the story. It is slightly embarrassing thus to amplify something that he only hinted at, and to resort to a matter-of-fact account that he did not want to give himself, but it has to be done if one wants to interpret the story. This, then, is what I suppose to have happened:

Like the other two sailors, Vickery came to New Zealand, where he met Mrs Bathurst at her hotel. They had a love affair. Once she had fallen for him she was completely obsessed by her love for him, as a woman of her generous habit of giving all she had would be. Hence the attitude to her many sailor admirers described earlier in the book; the easy and tolerant way in which she fended off their approaches, which she could afford because her affections were so completely centred on another man. Hence, perhaps, also the 'blindish look' twice attributed to her.

The wrong that Vickery did her was that he did not tell her that he had a wife, and allowed her to believe that he would marry her. Some time after 1901 (when Pritchard last saw her in New Zealand) she went to London to join him. At that time, Vickery was still living with his wife, for, as we have already been told, she died in childbed six weeks after he came out to South Africa. Published early in 1904, the story must have been written some time before. It takes place after the Boer War ended in May 1902, as otherwise Vickery could not have wandered about the country as he did; but not long after, as evidenced by the ammunition which he was sent to dispatch from Bloemfontein— there would not be naval ammunition there in peace-time. That Kipling took pains to indicate dates (for the beer-bottle incident and Mrs Vickery's death) that would be irrelevant if not meant as clues is surely significant.

Mrs Bathurst has thus come from the other end of the world to find her lover. As the film shows her, she has just arrived and is literally looking for him. She finds him, and now learns for the first time that he is a married man, and that his wife is expecting a baby, and finds that he refuses to break up his marriage. The earlier reference to his fifteen-year-old daughter is another piece of information contributing to show the strength of his domestic ties. What we have already learnt about Vickery indicates that this is how he would react in such a crisis: a stolid and prosaic person, punctilious about his duties and ambitious to be 'genteel', a conformer, not a man likely to take a step that would present him in a disreputable light. Realizing how she has been betrayed (and being the sort of woman who would anyhow refuse to steal another woman's husband) she kills herself, or dies of grief and humiliation.

It was said before that the film theme is the central one of the story. Kipling seized upon certain aspects of the new invention, viz. that a film could show, not only people in a distant country, but people who had died since it was photographed, and he used this to give a new twist to an old theme: *the haunting of a murderer by his victim*. This is what Vickery experiences in the cinema: he believes the dead woman is 'looking for him' again, in another and more sinister sense. The reason why he feels compelled to see the film every night is thus not that he cannot bear to miss one glimpse of a woman he loves, but the same compulsion that drives a murderer to revisit the scene of his crime. The ordeal of doing this is almost too horrible to be borne. He perspires with terror, and his face is 'white and crumply' like that of a foetus. In short, *Mrs Bathurst* is primarily *the story of a haunting*.

—C.A. Bodelsen, *Aspects of Kipling's Art* (New York: Barnes & Noble, 1964): pp 133–138.

ELLIOT GILBERT ON KIPLING'S USE OF APOSIOPESIS

[In this extract from his book on Kipling's short fiction, Gilbert compares the narrative technique used in "Mrs. Bathurst" to the classical rhetorical device of breaking off in the middle of a sentence.]

What happens in "Mrs. Bathurst" is, in the last analysis, a function of the work's structure.[24] All his life Kipling experimented with techniques for drawing readers into the heart of a story, for forcing them, if possible, to participate in the creative process itself. In "Mrs. Bathurst," among other stories, he succeeded in a way which was to damage his popularity and earn him a reputation for trickiness. But it was in just such stories as this that he was most brilliantly the innovator, most startlingly the stylist ahead of his time. Of "Mrs. Bathurst" it can accurately be said that the structure is inextricably bound up with the content. "Mrs. Bathurst" is a story about a group of storytellers who are trying to put together a story and discover its meaning. The story they are constructing is also the one the reader must construct, so that the two activities go on simultaneously. The group of four men gathered in the railroad car to spin yarns is, like the cinema and the episode of Boy Niven, a metaphor for Kipling's vision of life: the irrationality of the universe and man's need to find some order in it. When the four come together, each of them, unknown to the others, has certain disordered fragments of a story, quite meaningless in themselves. (It would be more accurate to say that three of the members of the group have these fragments. The fourth member, the writer, will one day record the incidents.) They begin to chat idly, in a random way, and slowly, as they talk, a story begins to emerge a little haltingly from the anecdotes and the broken images that each contributes to the general store of information.

Even when all the fragments have been assembled it is plain that significant information is missing. But it is also plain that with just the pieces available to them they have made an important discovery which leaves them silent and disturbed. They have, in fact, discovered the theme of their own story, and though that discovery is never discussed in so many words, the same fragments of information which led the four narrators to their understanding are available to guide the reader to the same conclusions. Indeed, it is because what the storytellers do is so much the model for what Kipling would have his readers do that such emphasis is placed on the "picture-frame" elements in "Mrs. Bathurst." The process of telling the story is as important to an understanding of the whole as the incidents of the story themselves.

In order to tell his story in the way he wanted to, Kipling had to abandon certain of the conventions of prose fiction, most notably the convention of redundancy. The usual story writer, in an effort to achieve immediate clarity, gives his readers too much information. Composing a conversation between two engineers, for example, he will have one say to the other, "Do you think there's much chance of getting a bridge across the river at this point?" Kipling, in a similar situation, would be content with "Well, what do you think?"—a line which might leave the casual reader mystified but which would seem clear enough, in context, to one who had been following the story closely.

The trouble with conventional dialogue is, in the first place, that people do not really talk in exposition. They say just enough to make themselves understood by the people they are addressing and do not behave as if they were aware of a large, unseen audience requiring to be kept informed. More important, such dialogue stands between the reader and the narrative, rejecting the reader's cooperation by assuring him that he will learn all there is to learn about the story without any effort on his part. In Kipling's dialogue there are few independently meaningful lines; meaning emerges from the total organization of what has gone before and what is to come. Description here is something more than decoration; it is a background against which individually obscure lines take on significance. A gesture will often finish a sentence. This kind of dialogue stretches the mind, requires, in Miss Tompkins' words, "a full participation of the imagination"[25] by readers who, like Pyecroft, recognize that seeing and hearing are not the only regulation aids to ascertaining facts.

There are many examples of this sort of dialogue in "Mrs. Bathurst." One toward the end of the story is representative. Hooper, speaking of his journey up-country on railroad business, says

> "I was up there a month ago relievin' a sick inspector, you see. He told me to look out for a couple of tramps in the teak."
>
> "Two?" Pyecroft said. "I don't envy that other man if—"

Pyecroft's aposiopesis, out of context, would be meaningless. It is probably meaningless, in any case, to casual readers of the story who have forgotten about Vickery's lunacy and murderous threats and Pyecroft's fear of being alone with the man. Those who have not forgotten are in a position to reconstruct the end of the sentence and so to participate, with the author and the four men in the railroad car, in the creation of the story.

The whole narrative may, in fact, be considered an extended example of aposiopesis. Hooper brings his hand to his waistcoat pocket, presumably to remove Vickery's teeth, but the hand comes away empty. Pyecroft seems on the verge of learning from Vickery's own lips the story of his affair with Mrs. Bathurst, but Vickery breaks off, saying, "The rest is silence." We are left to guess what exactly happened between Vickery and the captain, what Vickery did as a tramp up-country, and who his companion was. The tale of "Mrs. Bathurst," like Kipling's irrational universe, mocks our desire for reasonable explanations. Yet in the end, the theme of the story emerges clearly out of the calculated obscurity of the style.

Some aspects of that style are remarkable because of the way they foreshadow similar techniques in writers we are accustomed to thinking of as more serious. "Mrs. Bathurst" was published in 1904, some months before Leopold Bloom took his memorable walk through Dublin and many years before Joyce began to record the event. Yet this story uses a number of the narrative and structural devices which Joyce was to make famous in *Ulysses*. On the second page of "Mrs. Bathurst," for example, Hooper says

> "That reminds me," he felt in his waistcoat pocket, "I've got a curiosity for you from Wankies—beyond Bulawayo. It's more of a souvenir perhaps than—"

Here he is interrupted by the precipitate entrance of Pyecroft and Pritchard, and it is not till the very end of the story that we learn the significance of those words and that casual gesture. In *Ulysses*, Bloom, putting on his hat in the morning "peeped quickly inside the leather headband. White slip of paper. Quite safe." The explanation of this slip of paper comes only several episodes later when we read "His right hand came down into the bowl of his hat. His fingers found quickly a card behind the headband and transferred it to his waistcoat pocket." Still later we find Bloom handing this card in at the post office. As Stuart Gilbert points out, "These fragments would seem meaningless to a reader who had forgotten the earlier passages; the broken phrases assume an order only when 'an hypothesis is thrown among them.'"[26]

In his study of *Ulysses*, Gilbert further shows how each of the episodes in Joyce's book has, among other things, an art, a symbol and a "technic" of its own. Remarkably enough, "Mrs. Bathurst" may be analyzed in just this way. Its "technic" is the movie newsreel whose structure serves as a model for the structure of the story just as a fugue and a labyrinth give structure to two of the episodes in *Ulysses*. The symbol in "Mrs. Bathurst" is the storyteller, representing man's eternal quest for the meaning concealed in random events. And the art of the story is aposiopesis, the device of classical rhetoric which seeks, on every level of the narrative, to withhold the ultimate secret.

It is not intended that this comparison with *Ulysses* should be anything but suggestive. What it suggests is the concentrated creative energy which Kipling brought to bear on "Mrs. Bathurst," the self-consciousness, in the good sense of that word, of his art. And if there is some question about the necessity for such self-consciousness, we need only try to imagine this story told in more conventional terms. What would be missing would be precisely that tension, precisely that feverish sense of strain which Kipling deliberately sought to achieve. The style may be tortured and convoluted, but it is not tricky. It is exactly the right style for conveying to the reader both the subject and the theme of "Mrs. Bathurst."

NOTES

24. F.T. Cooper writes: "The whole strength of this story lies in the method of its telling. You hear it from the lips of stolid, callous naval men, rude of speech, coarse in their views of life in general and of women in particular. And through the medium of their very coarseness, their picturesque vulgarity, their lack of finer perceptions, you get an impression of a tragic drama which no amount of finer methods could have given." *Some English Story-Tellers*, p. 146.

25. Tompkins, p. 89.

26. Stuart Gilbert, *James Joyce's* Ulysses (New York, 1955), pp. 25–26.

—Elliot Gilbert, *The Good Kipling* (Athens: Ohio University Press, 1965): pp. 112–117.

NORA CROOK ON THE IDENTITY OF THE SECOND TRAMP

[Nora Crook is Professor of English at Anglia Polytechnic University in Cambridge, England. She is the author and/or editor of numerous articles on the Shelleys, as well as a full-length study of Kipling, which devotes an entire chapter to "Mrs. Bathurst." In the following excerpt, she proposes a controversial theory about the identity of the second tramp.]

More crucial (...) than the 'Is Mrs Bathurst dead?' problem, is the question of Vickery's companion. Who is the tramp? Since the story first started being discussed in the 1930s, readers have been divided into those who immediately assumed that it was Mrs Bathurst, the lightning-bolt standing for the fierce, lawless passion that has consumed them both, and those who as immediately assumed that it was a totally new character, a male drifter who just happened to be around. In Alan Sandison's opinion this is a blemish on an otherwise fine story: Kipling cheated in not allowing Hooper to say whether the figure was a man or Mrs Bathurst, 'for he was there and he saw them'.[21]

Those who want the tramp to be Mrs Bathurst say that it would not have been typical of Kipling to introduce a completely new and functionless character into such a tightly constructed story. (This receives some external support from the advice he gave Charles Warren Stoddard.[22]) Gilbert's reply was that the tramp had a function—to make the point that Vickery has committed passive suicide. When the lightning strikes, he stands up to attract it. Unless one had another figure by way of contrast (the dead tramp is squatting down), the point would not have been made. If so, this is a very clumsy device, and puzzling. What has the poor tramp done that he should be made to share Vickery's fate? Nothing, apparently, except to stray into Kipling's mind when stuck for a plot-mechanism. Gilbert, however, had a more powerful string to his bow, and one to which he was more committed. If the tramp had no function, the very gratuitousness of his appearance would be underlining the story's wider theme—man's search for meaning in a chaotic universe.[23] Unfortunately, the first bowstring gets in the way of the second. If the appearance of the tramp is supposed to be emblematic of the chaotic and random workings of the universe, then he really ought to have no discernible function at all. In any case, Kipling could surely have contrived a more arbitrary, less appropriate-seeming death for Vickery—one freer of associations with divine vengeance, the fires of passion or spontaneous combustion resulting from suppressed emotion (among the last words Pyecroft says to him are 'Consume your own smoke'). More importantly, any reading which is certain that the second corpse is not the dead Mrs Bathurst must reckon with features which have led readers to suppose that it is.

Chief among these is the use Kipling makes of the ballad 'The Honeysuckle and the Bee', which is sung by some picnickers immediately after Pritchard's 'Oh my Gawd!':

> On a summer afternoon, when the honeysuckle blooms,
> And all Nature seems at rest,
> Underneath the bower, 'mid the perfume of the flower
> Sat a maiden with the one she loves the best.

'This is clearly meant as an ironic curtain for the tale', Bodelsen commented, 'where the "bower" was a tropical wilderness, and the maiden and her lover two charred corpses'.[24] Bodelsen also saw in the positioning of the lovers in the song a correspondence with those of the corpses. 'One of 'em [Vickery] was standin' up by the dead-end of the siding an' the other was squatting down lookin' up at 'im, you see', which to Bodelsen suggested looking up with the assurance that he was forgiven. The phrase is certainly significant; Hooper repeats it, changing the wording slightly: 'like his mate squatting down an' watchin' him, both of 'em all wet in the rain'. The added words 'his mate' are also important. 'It is easily overlooked that [they] may at a pinch be applied to a woman, though the inspector no doubt thinks they are men', commented Bodelsen.[25] There are additional verbal links, not spotted by Bodelsen, between the bower and the wilderness. The 'Bee' corresponds to Mrs Bathurst, who is several times called 'Mrs B'. The name of the siding, M'Bindwe, suggests by aposiopesis the word 'bindweed'; the honeysuckle arbour, the traditional emblem of wedded love, is contrasted to 'bindweed', or convolvulus, also a twining plant, but scentless, predatory and emblematic of lawless passion. Holman Hunt uses it in *The Awakening Conscience* to symbolise the sterility of the kept mistress's love-nest; in Kipling's early poem 'Discovery' it is emblematic of the aftermath of 'dead love' (*EV*, p. 144).

Bodelsen also thought that Victor Prout's illustrations to the magazine version of the story were conclusive, claiming that the picture supposed to be of Hooper finding the bodies showed an unquestionably feminine figure. Kipling would never have allowed it through, he argued, if it was untrue to the intentions of his story. Unfortunately the available evidence points to Kipling having no control over magazine illustrations, and there is one known case of an illustrator ludicrously misreading his text.[26] Moreover, the charred tramp looks rather more masculine than feminine and the hands do not match those of Mrs Bathurst behind the bar. In my opinion this is a red herring, but two illustrations are reproduced in the plate section of this book that readers may judge for themselves.

However, Bodelsen saw that the tramp's corpse could not be that of Mrs Bathurst. How had she got there? Was she in men's clothes, and, if so, why? But in any case his argument required that she was dead. Yet he found it impossible to ignore the pointers that in some sense the tramp *was* Mrs Bathurst, and came up with the following ingenious shifts. One was that on the naturalistic level the dead tramp was indeed a chance-met male companion, but that at the moment of death he supernaturally 'became' Mrs Bathurst. Her soul had entered his body, so that Vickery and she could be together for all eternity. Bodelsen produced a naturalistic alternative: 'Vickery had a hallucination by which he believes that the tramp is Mrs Bathurst's ghost.'[27] Either way, Vickery died with the assurance that he had been saved at the last moment.

One wonders why it was necessary in order that the souls of Mrs Bathurst and Vickery should be reunited in the afterlife that her disembodied spirit should have to descend into a body again, even for a split second—the 'moment of death'.[28] Or why Vickery should imagine that the tramp was Mrs Bathurst's *ghost*. Since the tramp was material enough, it is more plausible that he would have imagined that his companion was Mrs Bathurst's *reincarnation*. All things considered, Bodelsen's explanation does not hold together. Nevertheless, the very difficulties that his theory presents lead to what I consider to be the answer.

Vickery leaves Cape Town 'happyish' and saying to Pyecroft, 'Phyllis's Circus will be performing at Worcester tomorrow night. So I shall see 'er yet once again' (*TD*, p. 361). This shows that he intends to follow the circus for as long as he can. The film show goes on an 'up-country' tour—Hooper has seen it when he was there (p. 353)—so it has gone north by way of the Southern Africa railway system. This explains why Vickery has gone as far as Bulawayo, the last big town on the railway line and a likely place for the circus to have turned round and headed back south. But when Vickery dies he is destitute, living on hand-outs from the railway folk. Clearly, there came a point where he ran out of money and could no longer afford even the 'tickey' (threepence) which readers have been told was the cheapest entrance fee. They have also been warned that 'deprived of 'is stimulant'—that is, unable to see the film—he is likely to commit a violent crime. Pyecroft is afraid that 'he might react on me, so to say, with a hatchet' (p. 360).

When Vickery runs out of money, then, he is in the very state which makes Pyecroft fearful for his own safety. But the attitude of the corpses shows that he has not murdered his companion. There is, however, another violent act which someone in his position might commit, especially if, deprived of the film (''is stimulus'), he had filled the void with his own fantasies and come to mistake his 'mate' for his dead mistress restored to life. This is sodomy, which in 1904 was a crime. Vickery and his companion standing in the 'dead end' of the siding would then have both participated and hence both incurred the biblical punishment— destruction by fire from heaven, the fate of Sodom and Gomorrah and of those who 'go after strange flesh' (see Genesis 19:24; Jude 7). Vickery, then, has been struck not by accident nor even by Aphrodite but by the Wrath of God.

21. Gilbert, p. 110; Sandison, p. 194.

22. C. W. Stoddard quoting RK during the Naulakha period: 'Do not, if possible, create a completely new set of characters to fill yacht in last chapter, but gather in people mentioned incidentally all along the book; thus the reader has not to meet new people late in the day' (Orel, n, 214).

23. Gilbert, p. 108.

24. Bodelsen, p. 141.

25. Ibid., p. 144.

26. Bodelsen, pp. 153–4. Kipling to Haggard, 1905: 'Pity one can't sprinkle lime over illustrators—same as slugs' (Cohen, p. 59). 'With the Night Mail' was the sufferer. See Lewis, pp. 36–8.

27. Bodelsen, p. 145n.

28. Swinton (pp. 64–5) proposed a corporeal spirit which could be struck by lightning and buried. This is stretching the concept of 'spirit' a little far.

—Nora Crook, *Kipling's Myths of Love and Death* (London: Macmillan, 1989): pp. 68–71.

DAVID LODGE ON STORY AND DISCOURSE

[David Lodge is a novelist, critic, and honorary Professor of Modern English Literature at the University of Birmingham. Author of eleven novels, including *Think* (2001), *Nice Work* (1988), and *Small World* (1984), he has also written extensively on modern literature. In this excerpt, Lodge deconstructs the story with a bit of modern "narratological" theory.]

If Rudyard Kipling is not usually thought of as a modern writer in the sense of modernist, it is because his work seems, superficially, to belong to a familiar and traditional kind of story-telling discourse, in which a lucid, literary, and reassuringly 'normal' authorial narration frames and judges the colourful speech of characters who belong to distinct and recognisable social and ethnic types. This impression is, however, misleading. It is true that Kipling does not indulge in the kind of stylistic experiment by means of which writers like Joyce, Woolf and Lawrence attempted to render the workings of subjective consciousness and the unconscious. But the relationship between the story and the telling of it in Kipling's work is often highly unorthodox, making it as teasingly ambiguous, as difficult and 'polysemous' as that of the acknowledged modern masters.

The short story 'Mrs Bathurst' is a particularly striking instance of this aspect of Kipling's art, one which has fascinated and, on occasion, exasperated several generations of his readers. In what follows, I aim, not to provide a new or definitive solution to its enigmas, but rather, by bringing to bear upon it the apparatus of modern narratological theory, to uncover the means by which these enigmas are generated, and thus to throw light on the production of meaning in modern narrative in general. What such a study of the story shows, is that, paradoxically, indeterminacy of meaning leads to an increase of meaning, because it demands more interpretative effort by the reader than does traditional narrative. (...)

'Mrs Bathurst' is essentially a mystery story. The basic narrative questions it raises belong to the order of mystery or enigma; why did Vickery desert within eighteen months of qualifying for pensioned retirement? What passed between him and Mrs Bathurst? What became of them subsequently? We get only partial answers to these questions. We discover that he was on the verge of losing his sanity at the time of his desertion, evidently because of despair or guilt about his relationship with Mrs Bathurst, which, since he was married until very recently, was in some degree illicit; and we are given convincing evidence that he died, struck by lightning in a teak forest in the South African interior, in the company of an unidentified second person. Even these partial answers are elaborately delayed. Not only that, but it is a long time before we discover what the questions—the basic narrative questions—*are*, and therefore what the story is supposed to be *about*. There are a number of false starts to this story which has False Bay as its immediate setting: the story of the narrator's missed appointment with HMS *Peridot*; the story of Sergeant Pritchard and the maidservant who gave him a bottle of beer, mistaking him for someone called MacClean; the story of Boy Niven who led a party of British servicemen on a wild-goose chase in search of a nonexistent farm on an island off Vancouver in 1887. All of these stories, which are introduced with elaborate specificity as to time and place and proper names, all of which information the conscientious reader files away in the expectation that it is going to be significant, turn out not be *the* story at all, but part of the frame of the story. The Russian Formalists distinguished between what they called the *fabula* and *sjuzet* of narrative. The *fabula* is the raw material, the basic story stuff, the story as it would have been enacted in real time and space. The *sjuzet* is the actual narrative text in which that story is represented, with all the gaps, elisions, rearrangements, selections and distortions involved in that process. Seymour Chatman translates these terms as Story and Discourse.

In 'Mrs Bathurst' we have a text in which there is an enormous disparity between the story and the discourse. The most crucial parts of the story, those concerning the relationship between Vickery and Mrs Bathurst, are never actually represented or reported in the discourse, and are therefore irrecoverable. The discourse itself consists of the testimonies of Pyecroft, Pritchard and Hooper about such limited access as they had to the lives of Vickery and Mrs Bathurst: these testimonies are like pieces of a jigsaw puzzle, most of which is missing. The consequence of all this is to displace the attention of the reader from the story to the discourse—not merely to the rhetoric of the discourse (though this is certainly the case, and a characteristic effect of modern narrative) but also to what might be called the story of the discourse: that is, the story of the interaction of the men who are pooling their knowledge about Vickery and Mrs Bathurst. If the core story is one of mystery, we might say that the frame story is one of suspense: *will they solve the mystery? what object will Hooper produce from his pocket?* are the questions it raises. The answers are as inconclusive as the answers to the questions in the core story.

—David Lodge, "'Mrs Bathurst': Indeterminacy in Modern Narrative." *Kipling Considered* (New York: St. Martin's Press, 1989): pp. 71, 75–76.

[John Bayley was Warton Professor of English at Oxford from 1974 to 1992. Husband of novelist Iris Murdoch, he is the author of numerous works of fiction and nonfiction, including *Alice, Hand Luggage*, and *Elegy for Iris*. In the following excerpt, Bayley examines how the story manages to be effective despite its "overkill" of artifice.]

Overkill of a kind is a Kipling hallmark. His daemon seem to have the power of putting more in a tale than meets the eye. And this can either add to the dimension of its truth or falsity, or both together. The success of "Mrs. Bathurst" comes from the way all the stories it contains run away into nothing, leaving only the image. People love stories, which seem to give shape and meaning to uncertainties and vanishings; and the idea of "the story in it," which Kipling may have picked up from James, is played with by the poetry of the tale, its suggestion of great distances and small units—ships and boarding houses—with their constricted lives, emotions and fantasies. As so often in Kipling's best work there is an insistent weight of unmentioned event and destiny, as if in the background of "Recessional." "Far called, our navies melt away, / On dune and headland sinks the fire." Incongruous but harmonious with this are what "They" calls "cross-sections of remote and incomprehensible lives through which we raced at right angles." The burden of falsity is placed on these "lives" themselves, the characters whose version of events and people is simple-minded or platitudinous, crudely fascinated, pathetically obsessed.

Thus the various stories in "Mrs. Bathurst" start up and flicker out, "like a shadow jumping over a candle." The fantasy about his uncle's farm told by Boy Niven, in which Pyecroft and Pritchett and their mates once "believed," merges with the possible versions of what may have happened between Vickery and Mrs.

Bathurst. Did he promise to marry her? Did he do away with his own wife? Did he desert her, perhaps when she was pregnant? Did she then do away with herself? What was the story that he told the captain, which caused him to be sent on the assignment up country from which he deserted? Delighting the characters who obliquely refer to them, these lurid speculations hover over the pathetic reality of the story, caught in its one touching image, an image which involuntarily places and falsifies the "words of wisdom" uttered by the characters themselves. These are Hooper's, in his slow comment on a man in Vickery's seeming situation: "He goes crazy—or just saves himself"; and Pyecroft's verdict on Vickery's being a family man: "'ave you ever found these little things make much difference? Because I haven't."

So "we all reflected together," to save the appearances, a process aided by the picnic party going past singing "The Honeysuckle and the Bee," a little song which invents a sufficiently happy story. But with subdued cunning Kipling's narrative returns to the story aborted right at the beginning, and joins it up with the other fragments. Hooper the railway man had found two tramps burned to a crisp by lightning, in a teak forest up the line, and one of them had some false teeth, "shining against the black," which he kept as a curio but never exhibits during the story. Two circumstances in this climactic event impress his auditors—and the reader. One is that there are two tramps, and one is squatting down and looking up at the other—"watchin' him"—a detail twice repeated. The other is that both are burned to charcoal, as if damned.

Belief in a story and belief in hell go together. The illustrator in the *Windsor Magazine*, in which the story first appeared, certainly seems to have believed, to the point of portraying the second tramp, looking up and watching, as an obvious female figure. C. A. Bodelsen, who in *Aspects of Kipling's Art* has most thoroughly investigated what its readers have made of the story, dismisses any notion that Kipling intended the second tramp to be Mrs. Bathurst. The story plays with its readers, parodying the marvelous power of a Kipling tale to "overbear unbelieving," the power which Kipling deploys with such relish in "Wireless"—which uses the Marconi transmission in the same way that "Mrs.

Bathurst" uses early cinema—or "On the Edge of the Evening." Because "Wireless" devotes all its ingenuity to the proposition "Wouldn't it be fascinating if? ..." it has no dimension apart from its own brilliant use of the Kipling authenticity effect. The different achievement in "Mrs. Bathurst"—and a very unusual one for Kipling—is to have things both ways. The reader partakes of the delicious and primitive terror which the characters and the "I" of the story are, as it were, hugging to themselves. Everyone likes the idea of lost souls. But, beyond this, the story's true vision is of size and littleness, the pathos of space, the small candles of human kindness and affection in the increasingly impersonal, mechanical, mixed-up world. Something in "Mrs. Bathurst" takes its place with the poetry of "The Dead," with Keats's vision at the back of "The Eve of St. Agnes." There is far more true Keats in the tale than when Kipling uses his poetry in "Wireless." Perhaps the shadow jumping over a candle was suggested by Madeline's taper, whose "little smoke in pallid moonshine died."

And yet Kipling spoils it. Indeed it may be an important if uncovenanted part of his general aesthetic effect to spoil things. Not that he insinuates too much the notion of jest, of making for the reader an elaborate spoof of things. On the contrary, after the first paragraph, with its superb and vividly surreal setting of the scene—an opening characteristic of Kipling at his best—the story never quite picks up, as if the author's own interest had silently departed too early. This too seems an exaggeration of an impression not uncommon where the stories are concerned, especially the later ones: and at the same time Kipling's air of not taking his own anecdotes very seriously does not seem wholly deceptive. Hardness and flippancy are not simulated. All this produces a complex, nervy, all-too-human effect: the very opposite of Joyce's fluency and calm in "The Dead." "Mrs. Bathurst" seems determined to bring out and emphasise all the tiresomeness of Kipling's method (as one talks of a remarkable but tiresome personality) but the final impression it makes is quite different.

It is an important paradox for the art of the Kipling story. A true and impersonal sadness can exist behind the all-too-personal ebullience, as a lack of knowledge lies behind all the knowingness and all the pointedly completed anecdotes. Kipling's daemon, who is, naturally enough, a kind of super-Kipling, is not—as "Mrs. Bathurst" shows—the ultimate artist in these stories. By exploring its different modes of falsity the art shows the scale and point of truth. As we emerge, spellbound, it is both a natural and a proper response to feel of each tale: "I don't really believe a word of it." But "not to believe" is, with Kipling, a gripping as well as an enlightening experience, for it points us to that unexplained world which can be behind his artful unrealities.

—John Bayley, "The False Structure." *Critical Essays on Rudyard Kipling*, ed. Harold Orel (Boston: G.K. Hall & Co., 1989): pp. 150–152.

CLARE HANSON ON THE RELATIONSHIP BETWEEN IMAGE AND NARRATIVE

[Clare Hanson is Head of the Department of English and Drama at Loughborough University in Leicestershire, England. She is the author of *Short Stories and Short Fictions, 1880–1980* and *Re-Reading the Short Story*, among others. In the following excerpt she locates the story's attraction in its ability to arrest the reader and suspend time with haunting images.]

To the extent that narrative may be associated with over-manipulative impulses, we might say that it sometimes becomes desirable in Kipling's stories for narrative to be arrested or thwarted in some way, for closure to be resisted. This is the case with 'Mrs Bathurst', perhaps his most famous—and impenetrable—story. 'Mrs Bathurst' originated precisely in images, which Kipling describes with unusual fullness in his autobiography, *Something of Myself*:

All I carried away from the magic town of Auckland was the face and voice of a woman who sold me beer at a little hotel there. They stayed at the back of my head till ten years later when, in a local train of the Cape Town suburbs, I heard a petty officer from Simonstown telling a companion about a woman in New Zealand who 'never scrupled to help a lame duck or put her foot on a scorpion'. Then—precisely as the removal of the key-log in a timber-jam starts the whole pile—those words gave me the key to the face and voice at Auckland, and a tale called 'Mrs Bathurst' slid into my mind, smoothly and orderly as floating timber on a bank-high river.[13]

It remains impossible to summarise or penetrate fully the 'dark an' bloody mystery' which links the two key images in the story: the literal 'cinematograph' image of Mrs Bathurst arriving at metropolitan Paddington station, and the later, haunting description of two charcoaled, burnt-out figures at the 'dead end' of a railway siding in an obscure part of Southern Africa. Some critics have suggested that an element of the supernatural accounts for the puzzles in this story: certainly the supernatural is a device, if it can be called that, which Kipling frequently uses to question or subvert conventional narrative expectations of cause and effect.

'Mrs Bathurst' is perhaps the most striking example of the way in which a Kipling story may be held together precisely by a tension between image and narrative. The two dominant images of the story are foregrounded to a far greater extent than in 'Mary Postgate' or 'Dayspring Mishandled'. First, *à propos* of the image of Mrs Bathurst, great stress is laid on the fact that we are seeing her on screen, in an almost magical sense, and that our sense of her depends on distance. If she comes too near to us, she disappears:

> Then the doors opened an' the passengers came out an' the porters got the luggage—just like life. Only—only when any one came down too far towards us that was watchin', they walked right out o' the picture, so to speak. (*TD*, p. 360)

Secondly, the importance of the two burnt-out corpses in the bush is stressed from the start of the story: we immediately guess the connection between Vickery and the relics of a human body in Mr Hooper's pocket, and the potential link is insisted on until we come to the final image of the story—an image, or figure, which is described precisely in terms of a reversed or cancelled letter (narrative):

> 'But if he was all charcoal-like?' said Pritchard, shuddering.
> 'You know how writing shows up white on a burned letter? Well, it was like that, you see. We buried 'em in the teak and I kept ... But he was a friend of you two gentlemen, you see.' (ibid., p. 369)

Working 'against' these resistant, mysterious images is a drive to establish narrative truth on the part of both readers and characters in the story. There is a strong desire for narrative coherence in the four characters/narrators; Pritchard and Pyecroft, after all, spend the first part of the story piecing together and concluding narratives about other seamen they have known, only to jump down Mr Hooper's throat when he displays an indecent haste to establish the connection between the relics in his pocket and Vickery, thereby showing 'such a peculiar, or I should rather say, such a *bloomin'* curiosity in identification marks' (ibid., p. 353).

The story ends inconclusively, leaving us, as readers, with a curious sense of relief, as if we, like Pritchard, are like children who need to 'shut out' the potential 'ugliness' of this narrative, and who wish to do this, in part, from an impulse toward delicacy (ibid., p. 369).

I have suggested that the short story is a form more closely associated with states of dream or fantasy than is the novel, which after all deals with the 'real' social world, with all its oppressions and obligations. In the short story the forces of desire most often find their fullest expression through mysterious, indecipherable images—for example the images in 'Mrs Bathurst' described above, or the image of the blue hotel in the story of that name by Stephen Crane. Further, I would suggest that one of the characteristics of the short story form (and particularly of Kipling's stories) is the frequent *impedence* of narrative through the interposition of essentially static images which 'freeze' or 'murder' narrative. The adversarial relation between image and narrative may be explained by the fact that the image (even the image in words) negates language, with all its differences and deferrals; the image is itself 'the density within which what I am talking about retires from view'. Language, or narrative, cannot attain such fullness of expression/identification with desire; it is by its very nature un-full, partial, analytic, concerned with endlessly (extensively) multiplying logical and causal relations.

Kipling's choice of title for his last collection of stories is particularly revealing in this light. The title is, and reflects, a paradox. For, as we have seen, in the short story it is the acceptance of limits, or bounds, on both the writer's and the reader's part, which makes the story free to express desire—to 'stimulate the reader's fantasies'. Limit thus allows and makes for freedom, for renewal. But the title points, I think, to a still deeper paradox inherent in the form of Kipling's stories. It is, I suggest, the continual 'blocking' of narrative by the interposition of the image which makes these narratives attractive, makes us want to read on. The springs of narrative are endlessly renewed as the closure of narrative is endlessly postponed: image and narrative thus work together, 'hand in glove', to create the particular kind of tension which we associate with the work of Kipling—a tension which is almost 'beyond the pale'.

NOTES

13. Rudyard Kipling, *Something of Myself*, Sussex Edition, p. 135.

—Clare Hanson, "Limits and Renewals: the Meaning of Form in the Stories of Rudyard Kipling." *Kipling Considered*, ed. Phillip Mallett, (New York: St. Martin's Press, 1989): pp. 93–96.

Letters of Travel, 1913.

Songs from Books, 1913.

A Diversity of Creatures, 1917.

The Years Between, 1919.

Land and Sea Tales for Scouts and Guides, 1923.

The Irish Guards in the Great War, 1923.

Debits and Credits, 1926.

Brazilian Sketches, 1927.

Thy Servant a Dog, 1930.

Limits and Renewals, 1932.

Souvenirs of France, 1933.

Something of Myself, 1937.

Rudyard Kipling

Amis, Kingsley. *Rudyard Kipling and His World*. London: Thames & Hudson, 1975.

Bascom, Tim. "Secret Imperialism: The Reader's Response to the Narrator in 'The Man Who Would Be King'." *English Literature in Transition: 1880–1920* 31, no. 2 (1988).

Bauer, Helen Pike. *Rudyard Kipling: A Study of the Short Fiction*. New York: Twayne, 1994.

Beresford, G.C. *Schooldays with Kipling*. London: Gollancz, 1936.

Birkenhead, Lord. *Rudyard Kipling*. London: W. H. Allen, 1980.

Bloom, Harold, ed. *Rudyard Kipling*. New York: Chelsea House, 1987.

Bodelsen, C.A. *Aspects of Kipling's Art*. New York: Barnes & Noble, 1964.

Brown, Hilton. *Rudyard Kipling: A New Appreciation*. London: Hamish Hamilton, 1945.

Carrington, Charles. *Rudyard Kipling: His Life and Work*. London: Macmillan, 1955.

Cornell, Louis L. *Kipling in India*. New York: St. Martin's Press, 1966.

Crook, Nora. *Kipling's Myths of Love and Death*. London: Macmillan, 1989.

Dobree, Bonomy. *Rudyard Kipling: Realist and Fabulist*. London: Oxford University Press, 1972.

Draudt, Manfred. "Reality or Delusion? Narrative Technique and Meaning in Kipling's *The Man Who Would Be King*." *English Studies* 65, no. 4 (August 1984).

Dunsterville, L.C. *Stalky's Reminiscences*. London: Cape, 1928.

Eliot, T.S. *A Choice of Kipling's Verse*. London: Faber, 1941.

Fussell, Paul. "Irony, Freemasonry, and Humane Ethics in Kipling's 'The Man Who Would Be King.'" *Journal of English Literary History* 25 (1958).

Gilbert, Elliot L. "What Happens in 'Mrs. Bathurst'." *PMLA* Vol. 77:4 (September 1962).

————. *The Good Kipling*. Athens: Ohio University Press, 1965.

————, ed. *Kipling and the Critics*. New York: New York University Press, 1965.

————. "Silence and Survival in Rudyard Kipling's Art and Life." *English Literature in Transition* 29, no. 2 (1986).

Gilmour, David. *The Long Recessional: The Imperial Life of Rudyard Kipling*. New York: Farrar, Straus and Giroux, 2002.

Green, Roger Lancelyn. *Kipling and the Children*. London: Elek Books, 1965.

————, ed. *Kipling: The Critical Heritage*. New York: Barnes and Noble, 1971.

Gross, John, ed. *Rudyard Kipling: The Man, His Work and His World*. London: Weidenfeld & Nicolson, 1972.

Harrison, James. *Rudyard Kipling*. Boston: Twayne, 1982.

Hart, Walter. *Kipling the Story-Writer*. Berkeley: UC Press, 1918.

Hubel, Teresa. "'The Bride of His Country': Love, Marriage, and the Imperialist Paradox in the Indian Fiction of Sara Jeannette Duncan and Rudyard Kipling." *Ariel: A Review of International English Literature* 21, no. 1 (1990).

Jarrell, Randall. *Kipling, Auden & Co.: Essays and Reviews 1935-1964*. New York: Farrar, Straus & Giroux, 1961.

Karlin, Daniel, ed. *Rudyard Kipling*. Oxford: Oxford University Press, 1999.

Kemp, Sandra. *Kipling's Hidden Narratives*. Oxford: Basil Blackwell, 1988.

Lewis, Lisa A. F. "Technique and Experiment in 'Mrs. Bathurst'." *The Kipling Journal* Vol. 47 (December 1980).

Lycett, Andrew. *Rudyard Kipling*. London: Weidenfeld & Nicolson, 1999.

Mallett, Phillip. *Kipling Considered*. New York: St. Martin's Press, 1989.

Manley, Seon. *Rudyard Kipling: Creative Adventurer*. New York: Vanguard, 1965.

Mason, Philip. *Kipling: The Glass, the Shadow and the Fire*. London: Jonathon Cape, 1975.

————. "Two Puzzles." *The Kipling Journal* 62 (December 1988).

McBratney, John. *Imperial Subjects, Imperial Space: Rudyard*

Kipling's Fiction of the Native-Born. Columbus: Ohio State University Press, 2002.

McClure, John A. *Kipling and Conrad: The Colonial Fiction.* Cambridge: Harvard University Press, 1981.

Meyers, Jeffrey. "The Idea of Moral Authority in *The Man Who Would Be King.*" *Studies in English Literature 1500–1900* 8, no. 4 (Autumn 1968).

———. "Thoughts on 'Without Benefit of Clergy'." *The Kipling Journal* 36, no. 172 (1969).

Moore, Katharine. *Kipling and the White Man's Burden.* London: Faber, 1968.

Moore-Gilbert, B. J. *Kipling and "Orientalism."* London: Croom Helm, 1986.

Orel, Harold, ed. *Critical Essays on Rudyard Kipling.* Boston: G.K. Hall & Co., 1989.

Paffard, Mark. *Kipling's Indian Fiction.* London: Macmillan, 1989.

Page, Norman. *A Kipling Companion.* London: Macmillan, 1984.

Pollack, Oliver B. "'The Man Who Would Be King'." *The Kipling Journal* 46 (September 1979).

Rao, K. Bhaskara. *Rudyard Kipling's India.* Norman: University of Oklahoma Press, 1967.

Ricketts, Harry. *The Unforgiving Minute: A Life of Rudyard Kipling.* London: Chatto & Windus, 1999.

Rutherford, Andrew, ed. *Kipling's Mind and Art.* Stanford: Stanford University Press, 1964.

Seymour-Smith, Martin. *Rudyard Kipling.* London: Queen Anne Press, 1989.

Shahane, Vasant A. *Rudyard Kipling, Activist and Artist.* Carbondale: Southern Illinois University Press, 1973.

Shanks, Edward. *Rudyard Kipling: A Study in Literature and Political Ideas.* New York: Doubleday, Doran, 1940.

Stewart, J. I. M. *Rudyard Kipling.* New York: Dodd, Mead, 1966.

Sullivan, Zohreh T. *Narratives of Empire: The Fictions of Rudyard Kipling.* Cambridge: Cambridge University Press, 1993.

Tompkins, J.M.S. *The Art of Rudyard Kipling.* London: Methuen, 1959.

Williams, T.L. "The Tramps in Mrs Bathurst." *The Kipling Journal* 46 (December 1979).

Wilson, Angus. *The Strange Ride of Rudyard Kipling*. New York: Viking, 1978.

Young, W. Arthur & McGivering, John H. *A Kipling Dictionary*. New York: St. Martin's Press, 1967.

ACKNOWLEDGMENTS

"Irony, Freemasonry, and Humane Ethics in Kipling's 'The Man Who Would Be King'" by Paul Fussell. From the *Journal of English Literary History* 25 (1958). © 1958 by the Journal of English Literary History. Reprinted by permission.

Kipling in India by Louis L. Cornell (New York: St. Martin's Press, 1966). © 1966 by St. Martin's Press. Reprinted by permission.

"Framing and Distancing in Kipling's 'The Man Who Would Be King'" by Thomas A. Shippey and Michael Short. From *The Journal of Narrative Technique* 2, no. 2 (May 1972). © 1972 by *The Journal of Narrative Technique*. Reprinted by permission.

"Kipling and the Hoax" by Phillip Mallett. From *Kipling Considered*, ed. Phillip Mallett (New York: St. Martin's Press, 1989). ©1989 by St. Martin's Press. Reprinted by permission.

Narratives of Empire: The Fictions of Rudyard Kipling by Zohreh T. Sullivan (Cambridge: Cambridge University Press, 1993). © 1993 by Cambridge University Press. Reprinted by permission.

Rudyard Kipling: A Study of the Short Fiction by Helen Pike Bauer (New York: Twayne, 1994). © 1994 by Twayne Publishers. Reprinted by permission of The Gale Group.

The Art of Rudyard Kipling by J.M.S. Tompkins (London: Methuen, 1959). © 1959 by Methuen. Reprinted by permission.

"'Without Benefit of Clergy': A Farewell to Ritual" by Elliot Gilbert. From *Kipling and the Critics*, ed. Elliot Gilbert, (New York: New York University Press, 1965). © 1965 by New York University Press. Reprinted by permission.

"Thoughts on 'Without Benefit of Clergy'" by Jeffrey Meyers. From *The Kipling Journal* 36, no. 172 (1969). © 1969 by *The Kipling Journal*. Reprinted by permission.

Rudyard Kipling by James Harrison (Boston: Twayne, 1982). © 1982 by Twayne Publishers. Reprinted by permission of the Gale Group.

The Strange Ride of Rudyard Kipling by Angus Wilson (New York: Viking, 1978). © 1978 by Viking Press. Reprinted by permission.

Kipling and Conrad: The Colonial Fiction by John A. McClure (Cambridge: Harvard University Press, 1981). © 1981 by Harvard University Press. Reprinted by permission.

Imperial Subjects, Imperial Space: Rudyard Kipling's Fiction of the Native-Born by John McBratney (Columbus: Ohio State University Press, 2002). © 2002 by Ohio State University Press. Reprinted by permission.

Rudyard Kipling by Martin Seymour-Smith (London: Queen Anne Press, 1989). © 1989 by Queen Anne Press. Reprinted by permission.

Kipling: The Glass, the Shadow and the Fire by Philip Mason (London: Jonathon Cape, 1975). © 1975 by Jonathon Cape. Reprinted by permission.

Kipling's Hidden Narratives by Sandra Kemp (Oxford: Basil Blackwell, 1988). © 1988 by Basil Blackwell. Reprinted by permission.

Aspects of Kipling's Art by C.A. Bodelson (New York: Barnes & Noble, 1964). © 1964 by Barnes & Noble, Inc. Reprinted by permission.

The Good Kipling by Elliot Gilbert (Athens: Ohio University Press, 1965). © 1965 by Ohio University Press. Reprinted by permission.

Kipling's Myths of Love and Death by Nora Crook (London: Macmillan, 1989). © 1989 by Macmillan. Reprinted by permission.

"'Mrs Bathurst': Indeterminacy in Modern Narrative" by David Lodge. From *Kipling Considered* (New York: St. Martin's Press, 1989). © 1989 by St. Martin's Press. Reprinted by permission.

Themes and Ideas